The Changemaker Mindset

The Changemaker Mindset

How Innovation and Change Start with Inner Transformation

Ilja Grzeskowitz

wisdom tree

Layout Design: Jermaine Lau
Translation: Bernadette Geyer, Berlin | www.geyereditorial.com
Author Photo: Philip Reichwein

First published in India in 2020 by agreement with Mango Publishing Group

ISBN 978-81-8328-546-9

Published by
Wisdom Tree
4779/23, Ansari Road
Darya Ganj, New Delhi-110 002
Ph.: 011-23247966/67/68
wisdomtreebooks@gmail.com

Printed in India

For my family.

The most important people in my life.

TABLE OF CONTENTS

INTRO:

One Shot

Look. If you had one shot, or one opportunity.
To seize everything you ever wanted.
One moment.
Would you capture it, or just let it slip?
—Eminem, "Lose Yourself"

I am not a particularly esoteric person. And yet I deeply and firmly believe that every single person is on this earth for a specific reason. That we have to fulfill a task that only we can do, because we are blessed with a certain talent or a special gift. What I don't believe in, however, are coincidences.

Picture this. It's a beautiful morning in the summer of 2013. I'm driving through Los Angeles in my Dodge Challenger rental car, enjoying the relaxed atmosphere of one of my favorite cities in the world. On the radio is Eminem's hit *Lose Yourself*, whose words in the intro magically move me: *"If you had one shot, or one opportunity to seize everything you ever wanted. One moment. Would you capture it, or just let it slip?"* As I think hard about this question, I drive down Broadway and see a building that fascinates me because it's so untypical of the City of Angels. On a whim, I stop and look at the sign on the facade. It's the Bradbury Building, which was designed by George Wyman. He was a simple draftsman who was working for five dollars a week for the original architect, Sumner Hunt, when he was asked by the millionaire Lewis Bradbury if he wanted to design the planned building for him. After initial doubts, he finally agreed. And, although he had no training as an architect, nor any past projects for reference, he created a building that has shaped the cityscape for over a century now and is admired by professionals all over the world. Wyman used his one shot to make a difference that was to outlast his own life. But it was to be his only success in the field of architecture, because shortly after the completion of the Bradbury Building, he faded from view and did not plan another building of importance for the rest of his life.

This story probably would not have had such a magical effect on me if I had not had the Eminem song in my ear at the same time. Because George Wyman, the designer of the Bradbury Building, perfectly embodied the words that the rapper, whose birthname was Marshall Bruce Mathers, belted out into the microphone in his own inimitable way: *"Look. If you had one shot, or one opportunity, to seize everything you ever wanted. One moment. Would you capture it, or just let it slip?"* Since then, I've been fascinated with the "One Shot" idea. The thought is that each of us gets a special shot with which we can make a difference. Some use it, others initially let it pass by, and then there are those who don't even notice it. I am firmly convinced that each one of us has this bullet made available to us. Maybe it's even two or three. But always one that matters. That really counts. In business. In love. In life. And it's our task in life to figure out what we use it for.

Unfortunately, far too many people can be distracted by the beguiling but misleading messages of the sirens around them and by waiting for the perfect time to finally get started. But, unfortunately, it will never come. We have no backup life at our disposal that we can use if things don't work out with the first. There's also no dress rehearsal; instead, our lives are happening right now and in this moment. You too, dear reader, have a shot like this. You are in this world to make a difference, to touch other people, and lead a life that truly deserves that name. Whatever your specific task is, start implementing it today, or at least start searching for what it is. Put your bullet into the revolver. Set your sights on the target. And then fire and make a difference, as Wyman did with his building on Broadway in Los Angeles. In your own way. In your style. With your personality.

At this point, you might be asking the same question that first crossed my mind many years ago:

"Is there really a reason why I am in this world? And if so, how do I find it?"

For a long time, I waited in vain for an answer, for clarity, for any sign. But no matter how intensely I searched, I just couldn't find anything. Until I eventually came across a quote from Søren Kierkegaard, who aptly stated, "Life can only be understood backward, but it must be lived forward." It was exactly the same with me, and today I know that my one shot, my purpose, and my talent is to help people, businesses, and organizations use the power of personality as the number-one success factor to thrive in times of massive change.

In retrospect, I have to laugh about my search for this task, because dealing with people, understanding their motivations, and the talent to inspire those around me for change was my great strength at a young age. The signs were always there. I just didn't realize it. At the end of my time doing civil service, the head of the integrative kindergarten where I finished my service was quite astonished when I told her that I had decided to study economics and marketing. "But Ilja," she said, confused, "as sensitive as you are with children, you have to do something people-oriented." As Managing Director for Karstadt, Wertheim, and IKEA, I was particularly successful because I always put my employees first. Because I had teams by my side at various locations that would have walked through the fire for me. Additionally, in my work as a business coach and keynote speaker, the focus of my work is never on processes, theories, or models, but always on the individual with their distinct personality. Because I am firmly convinced of one fact:

Life is a mirror. We do not get what we want. We become who we are.

And that's exactly why the title of this book is *The Changemaker Mindset*. Because in this time of increasingly intense digitization of all areas of life, the return to personal relationships, team spirit, and the individual—with all their strengths and weaknesses—will be the most important success factor for the future. Although this is already my ninth book, it's a very special one for me. And maybe this book is "my one shot." It didn't originate on a drawing board, but the topic found me in an almost spiritual way. Over the past two years, I've been interviewed for countless podcasts, magazines, and other media. Very often, I was asked this question at the end: "Ilja, what important tip would you like to share with others?" Every time, without a moment's hesitation, I answered with the following sentence:

> Grow as a human being and invest in yourself. In your knowledge, your skills, and your expertise. The next few years

> will be marked by massive changes, increasing complexity, and general uncertainty. The only factor that you can influence yourself—from start to finish—is your individual personality. Your mindset. Develop it further and you'll be able to look to the future with optimism and self-trust, because you'll possess a deep sense of basic confidence in always having the necessary flexibility in thinking and acting, no matter what happens around you.

This is the distillation of my study of human behavior and the experiences of the last fifteen years. *The Changemaker Mindset* delves into the distinct aspects, and details the necessary steps. In the coming years, the human success factor will determine who is among the winners and who is among the losers. Only those who place individual personality—and all its strengths and weaknesses—at the center of all endeavors will be able to succeed in tomorrow's markets of uncertainty, disruption, and increasing complexity. This applies to our society, the economy, and especially, to you personally. And in case you're seeking clarity about your life's specific purpose, then I could wish for nothing more than that this book is the sign that brings you the desired clarity.

It is my absolute heartfelt desire to inspire you to find your individual path and to provide you with the best possible stimuli, ideas, and tools for the implementation of your first steps. In my daily work with my clients, I'm increasingly realizing how ripe the time is to allow radical humanity to enter into our communications and interactions with one another, and into the active shaping of the future over the next few years. It's time to do away with the old motivational methods based on *Tschakka Tschakka* (a term made famous by the Dutch motivational guru Emile Ratelband), "Harder, Faster, Stronger," and on extreme pressure. What's more important is that we finally talk about the truly significant things—purpose, values, and internal motivation—as the sources of our professional excellence and personal fulfillment.

Would you agree with me that most people simply have no inclination toward pointless activities, soul-destroying work processes, and frustrating tasks? A job today has to offer more than the guarantee of being able to pay for the monthly rent, the lease on the car, and the annual Mallorca holiday. (Sorry for the "party people" cliché, dear Mallorca, but you know how much I love your island off the beaten track.)

At the same time, more and more companies are realizing how important the sense of corporate culture has become. The times are long gone in which one was mainly looking for diligent worker bees who did their jobs without much thought, picked up their paychecks, and then drove home again. No, in an economic environment where there are many more jobs than motivated and highly skilled people, human resource managers with foresight look for something completely different: identification with the company, shared values, and the feeling that one's own actions are making a meaningful contribution to societal development.

What, does that sound too utopian to you? I'll admit it, the seedling of this trend is still very frail, and in many places, the reality still looks the way it did in the 1970s. But I've set out to change this situation. And because companies only change when the people change, my key message is:

The most important success factor of the future will be a radical human changemaker mindset.

I could never put it as well as former US President Barack Obama did: "Change will not come if we wait for some other person, or if we wait for some other time. We are the ones we've been waiting for. We are the change that we seek." As I read these words, I am tempted to applaud loudly. The world and the way we live, love, and work may change dramatically, but you can always rely on your personality, with all of its facets.

Let me repeat it again. In times of uncertainty, change, and transition, there is one constant that you can always rely on, and that is you. No matter what happens in the next few years—and believe me, a lot will happen—you will always be able to count on your skills, experience, and knowledge. The more the future is shaped by technical changes, disruptive developments, and digital complexity, the more decisive the human success factor will be in business, in society, and in our personal environments. Therefore, nothing will be nearly as important as investment in training, work on your personality, and constant growth. In this way, you'll gain an unprecedented level of security in uncertain times, simply because you are aware of your flexibility in thinking and acting.

Sound good? Then I'd like to give you an overview of what to expect in this book. In order to make reading it as pleasant as possible, I've based my development of its structure on one of my most important mottos, which you may recognize as the red thread of my work:

When the WHY is big enough, then the HOW and WHAT will follow on their own.

From this interrelationship, I have deduced the three Ps of Personal Development:

The three Ps of Personal Development are: Purpose. People. Persistence.

The Purpose, the People, and the Persistence. These are the most important components when it comes to getting from point A to point B—mentally or physically. What could be more obvious than to subdivide *The Changemaker Mindset* into three distinct sections based on these components? At the start, we want to think, philosophize, and consider things without restraint, then to deal with important models, effective methods, and the power of a real team, before we arrive at very concrete implementation strategies.

Part one—THE PURPOSE—is about why we do what we do and what really drives us. I will present you with bold ideas to challenge you to step off your usual paths and to reconsider what motivates you the most and how sustainable change works. You will learn why, from now on, you should stop doing anything without understanding your non-negotiable core principles. I will introduce you to my Core Needs Model and invite you to become acquainted with the Change Diamond. With these tools, you'll come to understand why some people seem to succeed in everything, while others fail against even the slightest challenge.

In the second part—THE PEOPLE—we'll look together at why nobody wins alone, why your inner circle is therefore a critical success factor, and how to optimize its setup. I'll explain to you why a focus on employees is more important today than just focusing on customers, and why the world needs more battery changers. In addition, I'd like to instigate a well-prepared motivation revolution.

The third and final part—THE PERSISTENCE—is all about concrete tools and tactics for implementation. With the "Smells Like Teen Spirit" Method, the Seven-Second Rule, and the art of critical thinking, I will introduce you to the best ways to take action, deal successfully with setbacks, and implement sustainable change. Above all, we'll address the most important question of all: what does success mean to you and how can you achieve it? Building on this, we'll conclude with my model, the Growth Staircase, which will hopefully serve you faithfully along the way in the future.

To make the structuring and implementation of the contents of this book as simple as possible, at the end of each chapter, I succinctly summarize the five most important ideas in the form of a Changemaker's Memo. My big wish is that, after reading this book, you will have a complete package of ideas, strategies, and concrete tools to make a lasting difference, in your business, in your team, or in your family at home. But allow me one brief note: in this book, I don't claim to have found the one sole truth. (Have you ever noticed that many critics are much more dogmatic than those they criticize?) I also don't claim that my ideas will be the magic bullet for every single person in this world. Nothing could be further from the truth. On the contrary, I am probably my own biggest critic, and screen my own thoughts very carefully. But I also know that the methods presented in this book bring about above-average results. Thousands of people have already used them to lead a self-determined life, to position their company for the future, or to be successful as part of a team—just look at the list of references on my website[1]. And that is why I am firmly convinced that the concepts in this book can also be very valuable for you, dear reader. I would also like to emphasize a unique selling point that can no longer be taken for granted without saying it: I have not copied or transcribed the ideas and contents of this book from anywhere but have based them on my countless experiences of the last fifteen years. During this time, I have worked in almost every industry with companies of all sizes and people from all walks of life. And in addition to all the differences, there were always striking similarities. I combined these insights with intensive research and scientific foundations and have processed them into a distillate, which I am happy to present to you here.

I'd like to encourage you from the start to critically question each of my ideas, put them to the test, and try them out in your everyday life. And if I can inspire you with my approach, then it would be fantastic if you'd then serve as an ambassador to carry the concept of radical humanity out into the world, so that we make an even bigger difference together. In my demo-reel video on YouTube, there's a sentence I say at the very end that I would also like share with you in this book:

"Let's change the world together. I'm in. Will you join me?"

Nothing in the world would do more to fill my heart with joy.

Let's get started. We have many bold ideas and a whole book ahead of us. A book for those who expect more from life than paying bills, going to a gray office every day, and doing a job that's more frustrating than fulfilling. I'm motivated from head to toe, and I look forward to making a difference with you. The time for dissatisfaction, irrelevance, and pessimism is over.

The world is ripe for more meaning.

For strong values.

For the human success factor in times of ever-increasing change.

For the changemaker mindset.

Shall we begin? I'm very thankful that you are giving me your most valuable thing: your time.

Sincerely yours,

Ilja Grzeskowitz

Berlin, Lisbon, and London, 2018

PART 1

The Purpose

CHAPTER 1:

The Change Loop

Out past the cornfields where the woods got heavy,
Out in the back seat of my '60 Chevy.
Workin' on mysteries without any clues
—Workin' on our night moves.

—Bob Seeger, "Night Moves"

I had to overcome the most difficult situation of my professional career in 2004. Many of my colleagues at that time spoke of a suicide mission, while my superiors said it was a great chance to "earn my spurs." The task was as simple as it was challenging. As a project manager, I was to transform what was once the most successful department store in Berlin—the time-honored Hertie on Karl-Marx-Strasse in Berlin's Neukölln district—into an outlet center, in which the company wanted to sell old and discontinued stock from its German stores. It was a last-ditch effort to save the site. At the beginning of the 1990s, more than 1,200 employees worked in the more than 430,000-square-foot department store, and sales went straight through the roof after the Berlin Wall was opened. But over the years, economic decline affected not just Neukölln, but also the Hertie department store.

As a result, on my first day, the remaining 120 employees were desperately trying to stop the slump in sales, which had been declining by more than 20 percent per year for a long time. However, it was a hopeless struggle, because the decline was already too far advanced. Entire departments had been closed for a long time, and fewer and fewer customers were getting lost in the department store, whose atmosphere sometimes reminded one of a ghost town. So now I'm standing in a musty conference room, and in front of me are the six remaining department heads, looking at me with anxious eyes. The incumbent managing director is just a few weeks away from his retirement and makes no secret of his opinion as he introduces me to the team. "Ladies and gentlemen, may I introduce to you Mr. Grzeskowitz. He's here to kill our department store and turn it into a bargain center. I think the decision is completely wrong, but the young people always think they know everything better."

Boom. Can you imagine how I felt? Although I was just the bearer of the new concept, I felt all the anger and pent-up hopelessness of the people gathered there. As well as I could, I focused on the opportunities, presented my ideas for rescuing the site, and tried to reach the hearts of my future employees. This was followed by a heated discussion, which was characterized by many questions and interjections. But it was a single sentence that to this day has burned in my memory. Mr. Spencer (which is not his real name), the department head for the second floor (responsibilities for individual departments, like in other stores, had not existed for a long time), got up, looked me straight in the eye and said, "Don't you understand, Mr. Grzeskowitz? We can't use these new ideas here, because then our department store will die. But we don't want to die. We want to live!"

It was a sentence that hit me like a thunderbolt. And he exemplifies the big dilemma that changes bring. Mr. Leopold made this statement at a time when the patient, Hertie Neukölln, had been in the intensive care unit for years and—de facto—was already clinically dead. Yet the people involved resisted all alternatives like the devil resists holy water. They wanted everything to stay as it was, only they wanted the results to improve. This was a tragic attitude, because even if no one could say at that time whether the change would definitely save the location, the current sales, contribution margins, and forecasts spoke loud and clear: with the past strategies, the demise would only be postponed for a maximum of a few months. There were therefore only two possibilities: change or die.

Change or die. In times of ever-increasing change, we can either change—or we will die.

And therein lies the big dilemma. I am increasingly struck by the feeling that many people have grown weary of change. Because innovations are happening at a rapid pace, and some just feel overwhelmed. Because the word "new," especially in a business context, is often associated with leaner structures, staff reductions, and a shrinking of the personal workspace. Because everything that is "new" is often considered a threat to one's comfort zone. Because "new" often triggers an emotion that's the biggest enemy of innovation: fear. And that's a shame, because fear paralyzes you, slows your development, and sooner or later brings you to a standstill. For years now, I have been committed to fighting this neo-phobia. To putting you, dear reader, in the mood for change and to focusing on the huge opportunities concealed within the change. So, if you want to live your dreams, achieve goals, and be successful tomorrow, then it's essential to make the necessary changes today. It's important to make a radical paradigm shift. What do I mean by this? Please take a look at the following graphic.

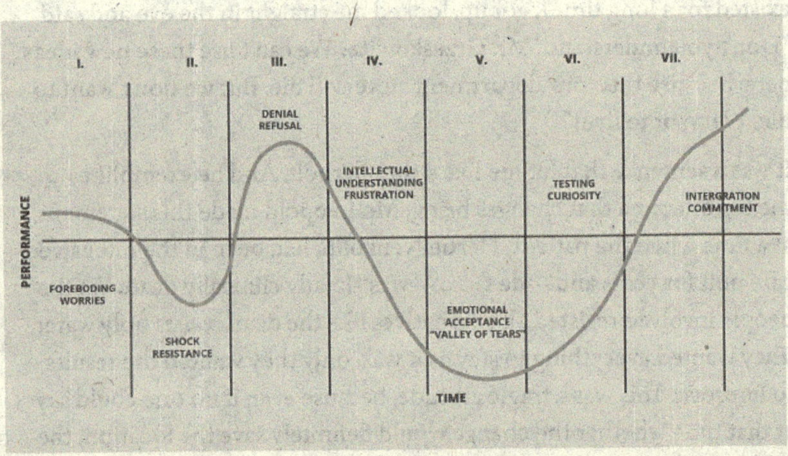

The Change Curve

You probably recognized this right away; it's based on the classic Change Curve that was developed by Elisabeth Kübler-Ross in the 1960s.2 As you might guess from its age, it's a model that has been taught for many years in seminars, workshops, and trainings. It's still used today as one of the standard tools in change management. Even senior management consultancies still use the Change Curve as their go-to model to help executives manage change processes with their teams. But here's the thing: it's not really relevant anymore, because the model has been overtaken in two important ways by reality. On the one hand, it's based on the assumption that change is always in response to external events, which is just not true today. Nowadays, we simply can't afford to be merely reactive, but we need to actively shape the future. The second obsolete assumption is that changes always have a beginning and an end. This may have been true in the past. There was a period of normality, with a change happening every few years, and you had a chance to rest for a while, in between, with the new normal. In his Three-Phases Model, Kurt Lewin called this "Unfreeze, Transition, Freeze." But these times are long gone, because we are dealing with conditions that no longer allow a change process to last for several years. Instead, change has become a perpetual, continuous state that keeps moving into our lives faster and more vigorously.

For this reason, I have developed my own model that incorporates these factors and meets the challenges of the next few years. I call it the Change Loop. I use the model not only in my work with individual entrepreneurs, managers, and executives, but also when I'm supporting teams and organizations. It works both on the individual personality level and for advancing corporate changes. As with any loop, there is no beginning or end, and each part plays an equally important role. Let's take a look at each of the Change Loop factors before I introduce you to my three most important predictions for the future.

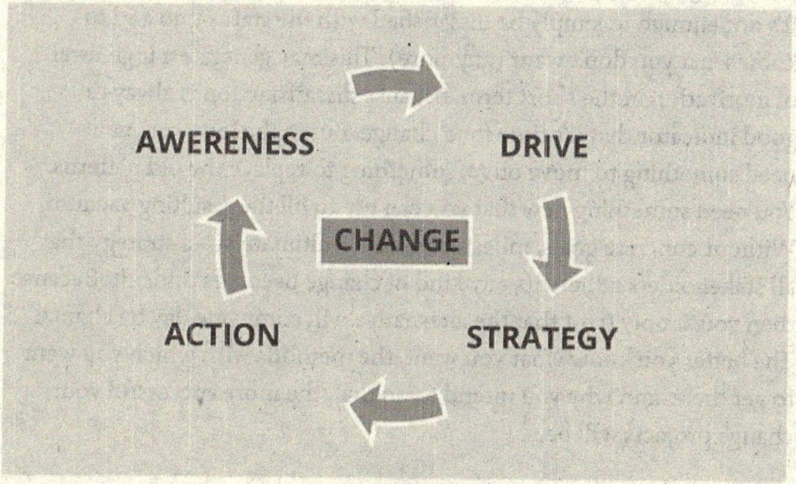

The Change Loop

Awareness

Because this point is so important, we'll go into it in greater depth in the section "Mindfulness, Baby!" For the moment, it should suffice to point out that a conscious approach to one's own thinking, acting, and functioning is indispensable for successful change. But be completely honest: how aware are you of the increasing complexity around you, your communication, your impact on other people, your role in your business, your degree of satisfaction in everyday life, and the level of responsibility that you are ready to take on? These are complex questions that are worth pondering a little longer.

Drive

Change is more intense, happens faster, and is more unpredictable today than it was just a few years ago. This leads to a certain resignation for many people, because they simply no longer feel like starting all over again and having to adapt, day in and day out, to the new conditions. If you do not have a sustainable and intrinsic drive when faced with these conditions, you will not be successful in the long term. In this book, we'll thoroughly explore how you can discover or develop this drive.

Strategy

This brings us to an extremely important factor for successful change. It's not enough to simply be dissatisfied with the status quo and to know what you don't want (anymore). This may generate a high level of motivation in the short term, because dissatisfaction is always a good indicator that it's time for a change. But in the long run, you need something to move on *to*, something to replace the old patterns. You need something new that you can use to fill the resulting vacuum. Without concrete goals, milestones, and—ultimately—a strategy that all stakeholders adhere to, any kind of change becomes difficult. Because then you simply trust that the alternative will come one day by chance. The better you know what you want, the methods with which you want to get there, and why you intend to do that, the more successful your change projects will be.

Action

It may seem strange to you that I included this stage of the transformation into the Change Loop; after all, it should go without saying, shouldn't it? However, in practice, this is not the case. If I had received just one cent for each announcement that was not implemented, I would be a multi-billionaire today. No, a remarkable skill for implementation is by no means a given. And because this step is absolutely essential to successful change, it gets a prominent place in my model. In the third section of this book, I will provide you with many practical tips, tricks, and tools to help you develop or expand your changemaker mentality.

A high degree of awareness, a powerful drive, a sustainable strategy, and a strong skill for implementation: these are the four crucial factors for successful change in times of increasing uncertainty. They reinforce each other, and unfortunately, you can't skip a step just because it might be too tedious for you. Additionally, the use of the Change Loop is not a one-time thing. You have to go back to the start and begin again. The deciding factor in this model has probably already jumped out at you. None of these four factors are dependent on the economy, external circumstances, or other people.

You alone have a 100 percent influence on your awareness, your drive, your strategy, and your actions.

And that is the reason why the subtitle of this book is "How Innovation and Change Start with Inner Transformation." Based on this insight, I'd like to introduce you to my three most important change theories for the years to come:

- **Change Theory Number 1**: We are merely at the forefront of changes that will dramatically alter the way we live, work, love, eat, or reside.
- **Change Theory Number 2**: Demographic trends, disruptive technologies such as artificial intelligence or robotics, as well as the digitization of all areas of life, will shake not only the working world, but our entire society.
- **Change Theory Number 3**: The most important success factor for the future will be the human being, because no artificial intelligence, no robot, and no software can ever replace things like personal relationships, empathy, or team spirit. Of course, this has implications for each one of us. It requires maximum readiness for responsibility and change, a reorientation of priorities, as well as a totally new and respectful coexistence.

The Change Loop, with its four components, will become the most important tool of the next few years—for you as a professional, as a family member, and as a changemaker. So let's take a closer look.

CHANGE OR DIE

Whether we like it or not, that's how it is. The year 2018—and those that follow, as well—has a clear motto: change or die! This applies to companies, brands, and organizations, but especially to us individually. Because, even if nobody knows exactly what the future will look like, one thing is as certain as the Amen in church: we have to change today in order to be successful tomorrow. Or, to put it more dramatically: anyone who doesn't jump on the train of change will play no role in the future, because they will be left all alone on the abandoned platform at the station. Does this statement rattle the edges of your comfort zone? Good, because our everyday lives will change massively in the next fifteen years. The way we live, love, eat, make friends, shop, consume, learn, work, and even die, will be dramatically different from what we know today.

But what awaits us in the future? Will our cars drive themselves? Will our intelligent refrigerators detect when we're out of butter and automatically trigger an order from our online shop of choice? Will we dine on noodles from a 3D printer in the near future? The chances are good, because this has been technically feasible for a while now. In my view, the following trends in particular will change our lives enormously in the next few years:

- The rapidly increasing proliferation of broadband internet keeps the world moving ever closer together.
- More and more knowledge is stored in the cloud. Never before has it been so easy to access information, know-how, and how-to instructions. A true innovation booster.
- Smartphones will become the organizational center for our entire life: lights, concerts, blood pressure measurement, room keys in hotels. There will be an app for everything.
- Robots and automated processes will assume tasks that we take for granted are handled by people today. This may even affect heart operations, which are performed much more precisely by robots

than by a chief physician. In particular, think about precision work, consultations, or assembly-line activities. The result: millions of jobs will become obsolete in the future, although at least as many new jobs will be created, most likely in industries that don't even exist today.

- Our behavior as consumers will adapt more to individual needs. On-demand services will be introduced in all areas of life. In the future, we'll want to be able to determine when, where, and above all, how we view, consume, or buy everything.
- Augmented reality—the computer-based broadening of our perception of reality will revolutionize the way we shop, date, have sex, present products, and go on vacation.
- Artificial intelligence will continue to become more intelligent. Even today, bots are able to successfully trade on the stock market and to train other bots. And there are Instagram algorithms that use your posted images to predict your suicide risk better than a human expert.

These are just a few examples; there are still a lot of other exciting future scenarios. Whatever developments await us, the digital age will ensure the greatest societal transformation since the Industrial Revolution—because the development of technology is no longer linear, but exponential. Take, for instance, the most popular smartphone in the world—the iPhone from Apple. It's been barely ten years since Steve Jobs debuted the first version of this revolutionary phone in a legendary keynote. Today we are already at version eight (or ten, the iPhone X), but I maintain that we are still at the very beginning of the technical possibilities.

Nevertheless, much of society acts like these developments don't exist at all. The public offices of our cities continue to worship the Form Gods by using paper, digitization is still being consistently ignored in many companies, and our children are being prepared for the challenges of the future with yesterday's methods. A good example? Gladly. My daughter Elisabeth's kindergarten purchased a computer with great fanfare for the children some time ago. This one had a tube monitor and was so bulky that extra space had to be set up for it. Of course, the teachers were not able to operate the newfangled device. But it was totally unnecessary, because the little tots belong to a generation that from a young age has grown up with iPads, smartphones, and laptops. No wonder, then, that little Theo proclaimed with conviction, "Ms. Miller, we're not interested in this old thing. But if you want, I'd be happy to bring in my mom's MacBook Pro on Monday."

An isolated case? Maybe, but more and more often I feel like the preparation of our children for the future is completely constrained by reality. My oldest daughter, Emma, has just entered seventh grade, and she can assume that in the future she'll have a profession that doesn't even exist today, because even the labor market is completely in flux due to digitization, demographic trends, and global networking. Millions of occupations will disappear in the future, and at least as many new jobs will be created. And how do the schools react? Innovation doesn't exist; instead, there's a standstill.[3] I was recently in my home town, Lübeck, to visit my old high school for an event. And, although I graduated from high school in 1994, it looked exactly as it did twenty-five years ago. Even one of my former teachers still wore a beige cable-knit pullover, just like he did when I was at school. And I have the legitimate suspicion that it might've even been the same one.

Everything changes, nothing stays the same. Change or die!

When I visit Emma in her classroom nowadays, I feel like I've traveled back in time. The furniture is still from the 1980s, they're still writing with chalk on a blackboard (and this is in the age of tablets, whiteboards, and knowledge stored in the cloud), and the curriculum prepares the students for long-obsolete career planning: high school diploma, apprenticeship/study, job in a single company, and then retire at sixty-five and collect a pension. But those days, and that concept of a life trajectory, are long gone. Today, those with high potential follow the lucrative job offers around the globe, whole empires are controlled from the living room, and the majority of people have no desire to be sent back to the scrap heap of the mid-1960s.

Everything changes, nothing stays the same. And, just so we understand each other correctly, we're not talking about utopia here. All of these developments have long been the reality. In 2015, I gave a lecture at Tobit, a software company in Ahaus, Germany. There, in the middle of a flat landscape, the company founder and visionary, Tobias Groten, has created a technology campus that is second to none. Everything is high-tech, and there's a corporate beach club and even a nightclub. Part of the campus is also a hotel, which is available to both guests and employees. When I arrived on site, I desperately searched for the reception desk, until one of the employees pointed out my mistake, saying, "That's all on our app." And indeed, after I downloaded the software to my iPhone, I set up an account using my Facebook profile. Immediately, the app recognized that suite number seven was reserved for me. There was no key, only a button in the app: Open Door. After I tapped it, the door opened, as if by magic. I felt like I was in a *Star Trek* episode. In the room itself, my iPhone acted as a control center on which everything was managed. And when I say "everything," I mean everything: lights, curtains, music, television (pardon me, of course it was an internet TV streaming service), the shower, and even room service.

It was really an impressive experience. After the check-out (needless to say, also via the app), I felt that I had just experienced the future. At the same time, I wondered if the traditional hotel industry is already prepared for these developments, or if it will be overrun in a few years. These kinds of examples can be found for every industry, including yours. Society, companies, and your personal workspace will be affected by the digital revolution. We will be confronted with problems that we can't really imagine today. And, at the same time, within these challenges lurk huge opportunities that are just waiting to be recognized and utilized by us.

At breakfast in the Tobit employee lounge, I had the opportunity to talk with a member of management about the company's innovative ideas. And this statement impressed me the most: "You know, Ilja, we haven't chosen these developments, but we always try to stay one step ahead of them. We simply look at the problems that arise and then work hard to find a suitable solution. Because, if we don't do it, someone else will." That's the mentality that makes the difference.

MINDFULNESS, BABY!

"You don't know what you don't know." This quotation is from the American linguist Noam Chomsky,[4] and it perfectly sums up the central element of this section. We consciously perceive only a small part of reality, because the great bulk of our thoughts, decisions, and actions take place on a subconscious level. As a rough estimate, you can assume that the conscious mind can process between five and nine pieces of information at the same time, whereas the capacity of the subconscious is infinite.[5] On one hand, this is very practical, because the resulting automatisms make everyday life a lot easier for us. Once we've learned how to ride a bike, that a hotplate can be damn hot, or that you open a door by pushing down on the latch, the corresponding program runs in the subconscious again and again, without requiring our conscious direction. The older we get, the more these habits shape our lives. Many of them are good, as well, and extremely useful. However, over time, we have also learned a huge number of unconscious thought patterns, decision-making strategies, and behaviors that have a negative impact, that can divert us from our goals, and even harm us.

And now we see the big dilemma. After all, how can you want to change, improve, or develop something that you're not aware of, because it's an automatic process in your subconscious? Okay, that was, of course, a rhetorical question, since it's simply impossible. Therefore, we've come to one of the most important sentences in this book. It seems very obvious, but if you truly internalize it to its full extent, it has the potential to dramatically improve your life. Have I built enough suspense? Very well then, here it comes now, the all-important sentence:

You can only change what you are aware of!

Sounds simple and logical, right? But if you assume that 99 percent of your thoughts, strategies, and behaviors happen unconsciously, then there's a lot of dynamite in that statement. Because, honestly, how much of your life do you lead in autopilot mode? How often do you do things only because you have always done so, because it's normal, or because everyone is doing it? How much do you really just "function," instead of doing your job with a high degree of awareness, shaping your everyday life, and communicating with people around you? Life only becomes really intense when you absorb it with all five senses and fully cherish each and every moment.

But what does this look like in reality? People rush from one meeting to the next, play with their children while "really quickly" preparing an important presentation for the boss on the side, and during their daily subway ride, they are so engrossed in playing Candy Crush on their smartphone that they wouldn't even notice if the other commuters around them were all naked. More and more often, I get the impression that everyday life has become so hectic that there is hardly any time left for conscious communication, genuine interest in the other person, and the high expectations we have for our own outcomes. You try to focus on one task, but your mind is already on the next telephone call, with tomorrow's customer, or in the weekly meeting (which you haven't actually prepared for). Sounds familiar, doesn't it?

The key to escaping this vicious circle of irrelevance, dissatisfaction, and mediocrity is awareness.

Only when we are completely mindful of both our outer and inner realities can we succeed in conveying the innumerable automatisms, habits, and strategies from the subconscious to the conscious surface, in order to change them. The biggest gift you can give to yourself it to turn off the autopilot and grab your life by the horns. Several years ago, I heard a sentence from my British colleague Nigel Risner that can serve as a mental beacon for you: "If you're in the room, be in the room." Yes, it pays to read that sentence several times and let it sink in. It's not enough to merely be physically in the room; we have to also be mentally there. Not just a little, but completely. One hundred percent.

The more mindful you are in a situation, the more self-determined you become. Because you are suddenly aware of things that would otherwise have rushed past you at top speed. Let's put it to the test; consciously ask yourself the following questions:

- What is my attitude like?
- What are my criteria for making decisions?
- Why do I do what I do?
- How do I act toward my fellow human beings and what do I notice about this?
- How do I know that I am happy and satisfied?
- How do I communicate with my employees and customers?
- Who thinks my thoughts?
- Which triggers always generate the same reaction for me?

Remember this as often as possible: you can only change what you are aware of! This applies to your communication, your habits, your decisions, your internal strategies, and especially your behavior. Therefore, I would like nothing more than to hear a decided "Oh yeah!" to mindfulness. Make the decision to only proceed consciously through life from now on and to pay attention to the alleged "little things." To critically question your everyday automatisms and to bravely look in the mirror. To enjoy life with all of your senses. The more that consciousness enters your everyday life, the more you will know what you do not know. But you can make the decision to change that. To grow as a person, to further develop yourself, and to become better. To lead a self-determined and contented life, instead of just functioning. I would like to conclude this section with the famous words of Hermann Hesse: "In all beginnings dwells a magic force for guarding us and helping us to live." Enjoy the beginning of a new era: the era of mindfulness.

STAY YOURSELF TO CHANGE YOURSELF

"Be yourself, no matter what they say!" I don't know if my boss back then had that wonderful song by Sting, "Englishman in New York," in his ear when he gave me the most important advice of my career: "Ilja, whatever you do in the future, the most important thing is that you dare to be yourself." I will never forget it. I nodded in agreement and thought, "Of course. Who else am I supposed to be?" And yet, in the years that followed, I was guided by just about everything and everyone, but not by my innermost needs, values, and principles. Because these processes took place unconsciously, I could not change them until I was more mindful of myself.

Due to fear of rejection and the urge for recognition, I have worn the most diverse masks and tried over and over again to please as many people as possible. It goes without saying that this kept me further and further away from myself. That's why your own personality is the most important factor for successful change. Only those who align themselves with their innermost needs can be as flexible as possible in their behavior. Or, to put it more clearly: a unique and stable personality is the best compass you can wish for in times of complex and intense change. We must stay ourselves, so we can change ourselves.

Stay yourself so you can change yourself.

It's worth taking a closer look at this wonderful construct called "personality" because, if we know how we really tick, then we also have a much better understanding of our behavior and our basic strategies in life. This makes any form of communication easier, which in turn, helps us succeed in all areas of life. But is it really possible to look inside a person and find out what their innermost needs are? The answer to that is a definite "Yes." This only works if you know what to watch for, though, because our outward behavior is always a mirror of our deepest motives. The first time I became fully aware of this relationship was many years ago, when I heard Tony Robbins speak about the Six Human Needs in a TED Talk.[6] Immediately, I was fascinated by the approach and combined the basic idea with other philosophies and schools of thought, such as Maslow's hierarchy of needs, the Satir categories, the DISC model, and other approaches to personality analysis. After many years of intensive study, my own Core Needs Model has emerged, which has since served as my preferred tool when working on changes with entrepreneurs.

The Core Needs Model

The basic idea behind the Core Needs Model is as follows: every person is driven by the same basic needs. Four of them are based on lack. If these are fulfilled, then there are two more, driven by personal growth. Before we take a closer look at the individual motives, I would first like to introduce you to the complete model, which I have summarized in the following figure.

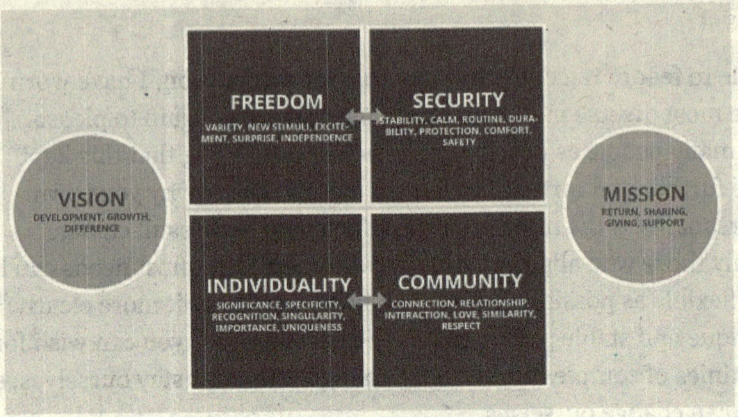

Core Needs Model

Now let's look at the core needs in detail.

1. *Core Need—Freedom*: One of our strongest internal drivers is freedom. We all need variety in our lives and enjoy the feeling we get from independence, surprises, and new stimuli. The typical characteristics are volatility, frequent changing of jobs or partners, reluctance to commit, and skill in experimentation and implementation. The core need in one sentence: *Nobody tells me what to do or not do.*
2. *Core Need—Security*: Equally intense is our need for security, the pursuit of continuity, stability, and consistency, with which we want to ensure peace, safety, and protection. The typical characteristics are routine, habits, hesitancy, shyness, reliability, and risk aversion. The core need in one sentence: *Everything should stay just the way it is.*
3. *Core Need—Individuality*: This is about the strong need for recognition, for meaning, and to highlight our uniqueness. Whether at work or at home, each of us wants to feel unique, important, and that we are making a difference. The typical characteristics are eye-catching clothing, extravagance, self-doubt, creativity, wanting to be in the spotlight, being loud and extroverted. The core need in one sentence: *Notice me, because I'm special.*
4. *Core Need—Community*: Similarly, we need affiliation with other people. We strive for similarities, connections, and relationships, and we long for love, respect, and affection. The typical characteristics are submission, striving for harmony, the sense of justice, keeping quiet, the desire to please everyone, putting the

needs of others above one's own. The core need in one sentence: *What can I do for you so that you love me?*

These are the four basic core needs of every human being. Yes, really for everyone. We all strive for freedom, security, individuality, and community, and we try to ensure specific needs through our behaviors. Of course, these processes are also automatic, so we are rarely conscious of our core needs. That sounds quite logical, doesn't it? But there are a few important points to keep in mind:

- Each person is driven by all four core needs. We try to satisfy these four motivations constantly, and almost always unconsciously, through our actions.
- The first two needs—"Freedom and Security"—are in conflict. We can't enjoy freedom without giving up security. And the feeling of security only exists if we sacrifice freedom for it.
- The same holds true for the next pair of needs, "Individuality and Community." To enjoy individual recognition, we need to break away from the community. On the other hand, community-based relationships only work if we forego the characteristic of uniqueness.
- All four basic needs are hierarchically at the same level, and none is better, more important, or more desirable than the others.
- At the same time, every person has a dominant core need that drives him more than the rest. This dominance can be very extreme, less extreme, or can be present merely as slight nuances.

It makes sense, therefore, to know your own dominating core need, as well as that of your fellow human beings. Why? It's very simple. If we know which motivation drives a person most, then not only can we understand them better, but also deal and communicate with them much better. Imagine that you have an employee whose core need is security. If you do not set firm parameters for this person, then they will quickly become dissatisfied. If, on the other hand, freedom is the most important motivation, then too many routines, instructions, or rules would be counterproductive. In both the workplace and in everyday personal life, the following applies:

The better you understand what drives you and your fellow human beings, the easier it is to reach your goals.

By now, it should come as no big surprise that even the core needs are not rational motivations but are doing their regular and reliable service on a subconscious level. It's no wonder—they are the result of our innermost desires, values, and dreams. Nevertheless, you can bring them to the surface fairly well and then—if desired, of course—change them. Be on the lookout for specific behaviors—in yourself and in other people—and ask yourself the following question:

"Which core need is supported by this?"

You'll be amazed at how often you'll start to chuckle. A friend posts selfies on Instagram with a more-than-average frequency? Clearly, this is because of their need for recognition. Your best friend has already started another project because he was bored? Say hello to freedom. Your colleague keeps saying *yes*, even though he really means *no*? Logically, this is the fear of rejection and a sign of his need for connection with other people. Someone has been dissatisfied with their job for years but has not dared to start something new? The need for security is simply stronger than the desire for change.

It is crucial that you recognize and fulfill your dominant core need.

These are just four examples out of thousands I've observed, and I'm sure you can immediately come up with many more from your everyday life. The more consciously you pay attention, the more you will find that virtually all behaviors serve to assure the four core needs of freedom, security, individuality, and community. This tetrad shows that the needs are all based on a lack that we try to balance out through our behavior. If we can succeed at this and, in particular, fulfill our dominant core need for the long term, then both of the "Growth Needs" will come into play.

1. *Growth Need—The Vision:* We humans are beings that have to grow. To be fulfilled and satisfied in life, it's not enough to lead a static existence in which we only maintain the status quo. And because of that, we strive to make a difference in life, to leave something significant behind, and to make a mark on the world. This is where the word *vision* comes into play. By this I mean a clear, attractive, and highly emotional picture of our own future, which magically attracts us, and summons us to action almost by itself. Our vision of life is very individual and serves as the North Star for personal development and perpetual growth as a human being.
2. *Growth Need—The Mission:* Real fulfillment is always experienced when our aspiration is not egocentric, but involves other people. This is exactly where the "Mission" comes in. At a subconscious level, we have a deep need to give something back, to share our success, and to support other people, whether it's in the form of a foundation, a social commitment, or simply by being there for our fellow human beings—not because we expect it to give us an advantage, but solely because there is nothing better than to look into bright eyes and smiling faces. The mission is bigger than us and comes into play only after we reach a certain level of growth.

A Brief Summary

Each person is driven by six core needs. Four of them are based on lack (Freedom, Security, Individuality, and Community, one of which is always dominant), which we try to compensate for by our behavior. Once we have permanently secured these four needs, the two growth needs—Vision and Mission—come into play. As a whole, the model also wonderfully describes why growth is so important to us as humans. Only when we first evolve as a person, and then, in the second step, give something back to others, do we experience this wonderful feeling of contentment that is so difficult to describe in words. And this is exactly why I like the Core Needs Model so much.

Not only do we better understand what makes us and others tick, but it explains so beautifully why personal development is not just an end in itself, but the necessary prerequisite for a life based on meaning and fulfillment.

The more we understand what really drives us and what our dominant basic need is, the easier it is for us to lead a life free from the expectations of others and to design our own future.

The motto is: *change or die.* And, at a time when conditions are becoming increasingly complex, technical developments are more rapid, and the pace of change is soaring, your individual personality is the only factor you can really rely on. The best part? You can influence this factor yourself from beginning to end.

Therefore, I would like to conclude the chapter with the words of Ralph Waldo Emerson, who wonderfully put these thoughts into a nutshell: "To be yourself in a world that is constantly trying to make you something else is the greatest accomplishment." So trust yourself. Listen to your inner voice and find out what really drives you. The more your work is based on the true core of your personality, the easier it will be for you to make necessary changes. In the next chapter, we'll take a close look at how you can best do that.

Changemaker's Memo:
The Five Big Ideas from This Chapter

1. The old Change Curve is outdated. Instead, the four elements of the Change Loop are critical to successful change: Awareness. Drive. Strategy. Action.
2. Everything changes, nothing stays the same. In times of perpetual change, the motto is: Change or die.
3. A person's ability to handle change will be the most important key skill of the future.
4. You can only change what you are aware of.
5. Use the Core Needs Model to employ your personality as a success factor.

CHAPTER 2

What's Important

Snow is cold, rain is wet
Chills my soul right to the marrow
I won't be happy till I see you alone again
'Til I'm home again and feeling right
—Carole King, "Home Again"

A frog and a scorpion are standing alongside a raging river. Because a bridge is nowhere to be seen, the scorpion asks, "Dear frog, I cannot swim. Would you carry me on your back to the other side of the river?"

The frog is outraged, "No! There's no way I will do such a thing. As soon as we get to the middle of the river, you'll jab me with your venomous stinger and we'll both die."

"But why should I do that?" replied the scorpion. "If I stab you, I will drown as well, and therefore would gain no benefit whatsoever."

The frog briefly thought this over and decided to take the scorpion across to the other shore. With one on the back of the other, they set off. But when they were in the middle of the river, the scorpion thrust its stinger into the frog and injected the deadly poison into its small body. With the last of its strength, the frog asked, "But why? Why did you do that? Now we will both die."

The answer came quickly. "I am a scorpion. It's simply who I am, and I can't help it." Seconds later, both were drowned.

Dear reader, you may be wondering why I'm beginning this chapter with such a sad and unusual anecdote. Quite simply, it's because we're all very similar to the scorpion. In each of us, there are dormant needs just waiting to reach the surface. We all have unfulfilled dreams, deeply hidden hopes, and defining values that want to be lived. But, unlike the scorpion from the fable, many people wait a very long time for the moment when they finally dare to give those things the necessary space.

And for some people, it never even happens. They live the way one does, align themselves with the expectations of others, and wear more or less comfortable masks. And that is tragic. Extremely tragic. This results in a deep dissatisfaction, because the internal needs are not in sync with the external actions.

I know what I'm talking about, because for far too long I lived a life that didn't make me happy. Ironically, I appeared quite successful from the outside. I was a managing director for a major retailer, made it pretty far up the corporate ladder when I was young, and in my future, many doors were open to me. There was just one problem: I had aligned myself with the goals, standards, and values of other people. Each day, I told myself a story that wasn't mine.[7]

We tell ourselves a story every day.
But who writes the script?

Although I played the lead role in the story that I called *life* back then, the script was written by others. And that meant that my innermost needs, dreams, and core values moved further and further away from my external circumstances. It may sound paradoxical, but the more successful I became outwardly, the more dissatisfied I became on the inside. Fortunately, in time, I understood what is really important. And it probably won't surprise you that I don't mean money, or the pursuit of possessions, or the accumulation of material status symbols. No. The Little Prince already knew that what is essential is invisible to the eye. Unfortunately, however, sometimes we humans need a very long time to come to this realization, because it's always the result of personal growth and the many small (and big) mistakes that we make along the way.

I still remember well the phase in my life when it was important for me to "show off" to the outside world. I collected status symbols, wore expensive clothes, and the admiration of other people was very important to me. It was my way, at the time, to assure the core need for recognition. But then came the time when I realized what really matters and is important. And for me, it was the realization that I am in this world to live my life according to my ideas. To orient myself toward my dreams, needs, and values. To no longer deny what is really important to me. To write my own story, to own it from beginning to end, and to positively influence other people. Call it what you want—Vision, Mission, or Realization—but I followed my inner call and, exactly ten years ago, I made the most important decision of my life. I quit my supposedly secure job as a senior executive and started my own business. With zero clients. Zero contacts. And financial reserves for three months.

Why am I telling you this? Because I often hear others say that it's easy for me to talk about change and risk when, after all, my circumstances were heavenly. Nothing could be further from the truth—my decision at that time was a big risk. The biggest of my life. But the inner fire that had been suppressed for so long was finally able to unfold its full power on the surface. And for the first time in my life, I had the feeling that the story I communicated on the outside every day was also my own. This brings me to an important question:

Who owns the story of your life?

Are you the producer, scriptwriter, and lead actor, all in one, or are you primarily guided by the expectations, goals, and standards of others? I'm well aware that it takes a lot of courage to give an honest answer to this question. More often than we'd like to admit to ourselves, we take certain ideas, opinions, and supposed correlations as given, simply because we've been told these things and repeated them often enough.
Here are a few examples:

- What's possible and what's impossible?
- What's politically correct and what's social conformity?
- What does ethically correct behavior look like?
- How do you set your goals? And which ones are really worthwhile?
- How much is enough?
- What standards apply to income, fees, or salaries?
- What does it take to be considered successful?
- What are your priorities in life?
- How can one be happy?

- What does the perfect life plan look like?

See what I mean? There is a good chance that a few, or more, of the answers you shot back are not yours. Because, every day, you tell a story that others have come up with for you. A courageous look in the mirror is, therefore, inevitable if you want to break out of this comfortable cage. It's the absolute prerequisite for everything that follows in this book. Because if you don't know exactly what's important, who you want to be, and what you imagine as a happy life, then who else should know? For this reason, a courageous look in the mirror is worthwhile. It's better to accept an uncomfortable realization than to live a life marked by indifference, mediocrity, and frustration. Therefore, I would like to inspire you—indeed, to call out to you in a loud voice:

Own your own story. Begin to lead a life of meaning. Make a difference.

How do you know whether you own your story? It's very simple. You do if your innermost needs, motivations, and values are in harmony with your outer actions. To help you approach this wonderful state, I'd like to ask some questions that will help you.

Ten Powerful Questions to Own the Story You Tell Yourself Each Day

1. Who do you want to be?
2. What do you want to do?
3. What values drive you?
4. What do you dream of?
5. Which principles are non-negotiable for you?
6. What kind of people do you want to have around you?
7. What purpose are you in this world for?
8. What difference will you make?
9. What is really important to you?
10. How does it all fit in with the story you tell yourself and others?

Start figuring out what makes you happy and what's really important. That means for you, not for someone else. You may need some time in order to do this, but this process is essential if you want to live a life of self-determination and personal freedom, where you express your most important inner needs, both in your job and in your everyday life, through your actions. Why? Because personal development is the basic requirement for any kind of success. Or, to put it more succinctly:

Only when you grow as a person can you become a better boss, parent, employee, colleague, salesperson, manager, or entrepreneur.

And it doesn't matter how exactly you imagine your own personal future. Everything starts with one of the most important questions: *What is really important to you?*

To help you with the answer, I'd like to introduce you to a concept that has the potential to dramatically increase your quality of life. I'm talking about a personal freedom plan.

THE PERSONAL FREEDOM PLAN

Toward the end of my studies in business administration, I hardly spent time anymore in the lecture hall (fortunately, we had a clever system for always being on the attendance list for the compulsory events). No wonder—firstly, because the content we were being taught was not really exciting. And secondly, because I had extremely interesting jobs as a student. In addition to interpreting for a Texan construction company, looking after Nigerian companies visiting gravel pits in rural northeast Germany and doing a cool job as a business development manager for a software company, I also worked as a business plan developer for young founders. There were certainly plenty of those in this time of the "New Economy," when everyone wanted to have a piece of the internet pie that was just emerging. Even then, I was fascinated by the depth to which a potential entrepreneur had to calculate his professional future and how detailed a plan he had to work out for the years to come. Professional development does not always go exactly according to plan, but the better prepared you are, the better your chances for a successful future. However, if you look at how most people plan their lives, you quickly come to a sobering realization: They don't! The "how, where, and with whom?" is usually the result of a chain of coincidences that have come about over time. You are not really happy or fortunate, but it's just the way it is. And that's why you settle for the dissatisfying status quo and become melancholy in the quiet moments, remembering all the dreams you once had when you were younger.

It breaks my heart again and again when I observe how my contemporaries make such detailed plans for their packaged holiday on the party beaches, the purchase of a new 3D television, or away-game trips for the upcoming soccer season, but passively leave their own lives to chance. I would therefore like to encourage you to actively shape your happiness and satisfaction, to grab the future by the horns, and to develop your personal freedom plan. The formula is as follows:

LP + BP = FP

Life Plan + Business Plan = Personal Freedom Plan

The combination of your dream life with a corresponding work life ultimately leads to a personal freedom that forms the basis for true fulfillment. "But Ilja, don't you always say that a happy life cannot be planned on a drawing board?" Yes, that's right. After all, John Lennon said, "Life is what happens to you while you're busy making other plans." Nevertheless, we should shape our future as actively as possible, according to our ideas and innermost needs, and align ourselves with what is really important to us. Therefore, we should deal with potential crises, setbacks, and other external factors when they happen, always aware that we will find a solution. Because what would the alternative look like? You can observe this day in and day out in your personal environment. Isn't that right? How many people do you know who let themselves be guided by other people's expectations, have a frustrating job, and have a very drab overall existence?

Start developing your personal freedom plan today.

When developing your personal freedom plan, the order is crucial. First comes the question, "How do I imagine my ideal life?" and then comes the appropriate career development. Unfortunately, reality is exactly the other way around in 99 percent of the cases. A person at some point chooses a certain profession, often by chance, and then adapts to it over the years. I, too, slipped into my career as a department store manager more by chance than from a conscious decision. And with the professional tasks came the corresponding lifestyle: Every one or two years a new branch, a new city, and a new social circle. That meant a completely new start each time, bringing with it the nagging uncertainty of never knowing exactly where I would be in the future. The location in which I worked and lived depended completely on the whims and decisions of my respective superiors. And since self-determination was one of my most important values, even back then, these circumstances led to an ever-increasing internal frustration. When I was young and single, this lifestyle could even be fun, but later, with the birth of my first daughter, I felt more profoundly that I had not imagined my life that way.

With each passing day, I felt more and more like a victim. A victim of external circumstances. A victim of my capricious bosses. And, in situations where everything seemed to be going against me, sometimes even like a victim of the whole universe. As is often the case, I had to save my life myself. One day, a businessman said something to me that burned into my cerebral cortex and flipped an inner switch. It is so important that I want to highlight it explicitly:

"You are not the victim of the universe, you are the universe!"

Even today, I still get goosebumps when I let those words work on me. As soon as we realize that only we, ourselves—and no one else—are responsible for fulfilling the design of our future, fascinating things suddenly happen. Because if you flip the switch and replace the victim attitude with an active "designer" mentality, then you're really ready to go. Now I suspect that some variant of the following objection is going through your head: "But Ilja, I'm just a simple sales rep/sales assistant/department manager. What kind of big change can I make?" Believe me, I understand this line of thinking only too well. I've thought it myself hundreds of times and then stowed my dreams away in a supposedly secure drawer. Yet, regardless of your current situation, you can always say, "Stop. This is where I draw the line. From now on, I will lead a life that reflects my innermost needs on the outside, as well." All it takes is a decision, because you are not a victim of the universe, you are the universe.

Which should you choose? Imagine me sitting in front of you, like Morpheus from the movie *The Matrix*, and offering you two pills. Choose the blue, then everything stays as it is. You remain blissfully ignorant and continue to believe what you are supposed to believe. You work diligently, like an ant, drive to your office every day, and weekends and holidays are among the few highlights in your otherwise rather drab everyday life. Or do you choose the red pill? Get ready for a fast roller-coaster ride through the rabbit hole we call life. Like Morpheus, I won't give you rose-tinted glasses to wear, nor will I make you any dubious promises. All I have to offer you is the beauty of the opportunities that are just waiting to be used by you.

The following three steps will enable you to lead a self-determined life of personal freedom.

Step 1: Define Your Life Plan

It all starts with your big, attractive vision for life. What should your everyday life look like? Which people do you want to live with, and where? Determine what's really important and then build everything else around that vision. At the same time, this is the question I'm asked most often after my presentations and events: "Ilja, I feel like it's time for a change, but how do I find my own personal vision?" I will admit that this isn't easy, because you can neither buy a plan from the grocery store, nor copy one from other people. Instead, it's the direct result of personal development. The more you grow as a person, the more you will feel inner clarity and perceive what counts and what makes you truly happy. If you are really serious about your vision, I'd like to invite you to complete a small exercise. It's very simple. Answer the following questions. Make sure you listen to the first response that comes to mind and write it down. Please don't look for rational reasons or socially acceptable expressions, and don't make evaluations. What we are looking for are the unconscious needs that speak to you whenever you feel a spontaneous impulse. Please write down these needs. And then answer the questions again tomorrow. And then again the day after that. For the next thirty days. You'll be surprised at how your clarity begins to grow during this time. To make things easier for you, I've divided the questions into four thematic blocks.

Thematic Block 1: Personal Vision Questions

- What do I wish for myself most of all?
- What would I do if I had sufficient time, funds, and resources at my disposal?
- What would I never do, no matter what anyone offered me?
- What else do I want to achieve in my life?
- What will I produce that will continue to exist, even after I have passed away?
- Which values play a crucial role in my life?
- What would I do if I had a guarantee that I would be successful?
- What do I want other people to remember me for?
- What do I want people to never say about me?

Thematic Block 2: Financial Vision Questions

- If money didn't matter, what would I do with my life?
- How much money would I have to earn to have the security I need?
- How much money would I have to earn to make real decisions?
- How much money would I have to earn to have real financial freedom?

Thematic Block 3: Professional Vision Questions

- What would I willingly do without payment?
- What can I do better than anyone else?
- What special talents and abilities do I have?
- What do I regularly do that is a complete waste of my talents and abilities?
- In which areas do others consider me better than I consider myself?
- What makes my eyes sparkle?
- In which activities do I gladly forget what time it is?

Thematic Block 4: Lifestyle Vision Questions

- What is the everyday life that I dream of?
- What bores me? What makes me happy?
- What gives me energy?
- What frustrates me and makes me unhappy?
- In which places do I truly flourish?
- Which people inspire me?
- If I knew I could not fail, what would I do?
- If I could be known and appreciated for one thing, what would that be?

Please be completely honest with yourself when answering these questions. I guarantee you that you will move a big step closer to your personal vision of life. The sole purpose of this exercise is for you to deal with your innermost needs. And I don't mean the ones you like to tell other people about simply because you feel they make you more popular. No, I'm talking about the ones that lie dormant deep inside you, just waiting to finally be lived by you. And these specific motivations, wishes, and dreams should form the foundation of your personal life plan, around which you can then build your professional future.

Step 2: Your Business Plan

Once you've developed a vision for your life, it's time to start a business or find a job that fits your dream life. This can be your own business but can also be your career as an employee. Let yourself be guided by what you imagine your dream job to be like. Would you like to work in an office, or do you want to have the flexibility to work from anywhere? Do you need fixed working hours or maximum freedom? Would you like to work together with colleagues as part of a team, or would you rather be completely alone? Whatever you wish for, one thing is especially important: think big, act courageously, but be sure to take this step only after defining your life plan. Again, radical honesty is necessary here. Be guided by your needs—not trends, the public's perception and judgement of you, or the opinions of others.

Step 3: Your Personal Freedom Plan

This phase is more than the sum of the life plan plus the business plan. It is your very personal declaration of independence. From this point on, you have only one task left: to enjoy your personal freedom and to be grateful for leading a life of meaning and professional fulfillment. Because, at the end of the day, it is self-determination that makes the decisive difference, and that is the linchpin of true happiness and deep contentment.

How did you do with the above exercises? I am well aware that many of the questions and steps can get down into the nitty-gritty. And, of course, it's not easy to change a lifestyle that has taken us from one day to the next, possibly over the course of many years. The important thing is that you think bravely, and then start on your way with small steps. In a time characterized by insecurity, uncertainty, and incalculable risks, self-determination has become a new source of security. Because in times of ever-increasing change, your personality—with all your talents, skills, and strengths—is the only factor that you can influence from start to finish. The more you love life and do your job with passion, the better you will succeed.

POSITIVE OBSESSION

I will never forget the day of my confirmation. Back then, I was a shy little thirteen-year-old boy who—dressed in a poorly fitting jacket—was to be accepted into the adult world, together with many other neighborhood children. After a seemingly endless confirmation period, we had to endure one last—and always dreadfully boring—mass before we were finally ready. The big party was going on, and each guest handed me their gift: an envelope in which there were bills—between twenty and a hundred marks. The sumptuous grand total would not remain in my possession for long, however, because I immediately invested it in a hi-fi tower, from which, three years later, a goosebumps-inducing riff by Kurt Cobain would sound—which I will go into intensely in Chapter 9. But I digress. The moment that I still remember most intensely today is a completely different one.

After drinking coffee with me, my father rose from his seat, dug out a folded slip of paper from his trouser pocket, and gave me a speech entitled, "All you need is love." Moved by his own words, his feelings overcame him after only a few seconds, and tears came to his eyes. Nevertheless, he bravely held on and used the Beatles' song title to give me a critical message for me to take on my life's path. "Son, whatever the future holds for you, the important thing is that you do what you love and spend time with people you love and who love you. Everything else is secondary and will fall into place." How right my father was.

All you need is love. Many years have passed since then, and I left the church long ago. Nevertheless, I still often think of my confirmation and the words of John Lennon, because they always remind me of what is really important in life. It is a love of life in all its facets and the people with whom we spend our time. Even in business, this most beautiful of all the emotions plays a big role. Whenever we love our job, our products, and especially our customers, we inevitably deliver above-average results. And the best part is that we can have a lot of fun at the same time. What exactly do I mean by that? I still like to recall when, for the first time, many years ago, I heard the saying, *"Imagine coming home in the evening and thinking: Wow! And I also get paid for that!"*

The results we achieve are the mirror of how much we love what we do every single day.

What you need to know is that, at that moment, I still had a job that did not really make me happy. Therefore, this statement seemed completely utopian and crazy to me. After all, I was often very excited about the end of the workday, because then I could finally do the things that filled my heart with joy. Only many years later, after a grand day full of euphoria as an independent entrepreneur, I walked through my front door and finally knew what an incredible effect this sentence actually has. And I decided that I would like to have that exact feeling every single day. This decision was followed by my own personal freedom plan, a lot of hard work, and an even greater number of mistakes. But I've made it, and I'm still grateful every day for being able to make money doing what I love—with all my heart—to do.

Since we are talking about business here, the word passion is likely to be a better fit, as it's the foundation of positive obsession, which in turn leads to above-average results. But if we leave the semantics aside, what I really want to convey is just how crucial a high emotional involvement is to professional fulfillment. And, obviously, I am aware that this is not accomplished with passion alone. To be really good at a job requires skill, diligence, persistence, commitment, and a great deal of talent. But without a passion for our profession, these qualities evaporate, because without the right topsoil, even the most beautiful flower cannot shine forth in its full glory. Fortunately, conversely, the same applies. The results we achieve in business are the direct reflection of how much we love what we do every single day. But you wouldn't believe how many people out there are doing a job for which they feel everything except passion. Would you agree with me? Life is simply too short to waste on a job that bores us at best, but in the worst case makes us feel frustrated and ill. Instead, we always flourish when what we do every day has a meaning and a deeper sense of purpose.

It's therefore time to make a Passion Check. What do you love about your job? If you can't think of anything straight away, that's normal. Often, these are things we don't even think about at first. Thus, I would encourage you to take a closer look. A passion for business and a love for work can have four different characteristics, which I call Love Factors.

Love Factor Number 1: You Love WHAT You Do in Your Job

It may surprise you, but this category is not only the weakest, but also the rarest. Of course, there are people who go into their occupation and would rather not do anything else the whole day. But this is not the case with the majority. I'd go so far as to say that three-quarters of what we all do every day is pretty boring. By the way, it's no different for me. The constant waiting at airports, missed trains, endless telephone conferences, the monthly bookkeeping, or the many lonely nights in anonymous hotels are among the things I do not like. But I love the one-quarter that is really cool—like speaking on the stages of the world or writing my books—so much that I'm willing to accept the tedious other stuff as part of the package. How about you? If you love what you do, then you are happy. And if not, that's not just not a problem, it's perfectly normal. Concentrate on the other three categories.

Love Factor Number 2: You Love HOW You Do Your Job

I'm a big fan of star chef Gordon Ramsay. On his television show, he regularly rescues ailing restaurants from impending bankruptcy. In addition to faulty concepts, lazy owners, and grubby kitchens, one thing annoys him again and again: when people do not cook with passion. Usually, Gordon then grabs his cooking smock and starts to rock the kitchen. "Cooking is like sex," he likes to say. "It takes passion for the preparation, a love for the products, and the ultimate palate orgasm awaits as a result." How right he is. I admire all people who approach their jobs with such a passion. Painters swinging their brushes as if they were Salvador Dali. Accountants juggling numbers as if there were nothing better in the world. Or teachers who treat their students as if each one of them was a very special gift to the world. Because that's exactly what every single child is! So, whatever kind of job you have, do the work with an infectious passion. Because if you love how you do something, then even the smallest task acquires a great significance.

Love Factor Number 3: You Love Those FOR WHOM You Do Your Job

This driver can unleash a tremendous power. It may well be that you can't summon up a great passion for the WHAT or the HOW. But you still do your job because you love those you are doing it for. Because other people benefit from your work. This can be your children, but also your colleagues, your family, the company, or your customers. Want an example? Whenever I have a small dip in my motivation, I simply need to look at the picture on my desk. As soon as I look at the bright faces of my two daughters, Emma and Elisabeth, I feel my inner fire again, because I know who I'm giving my all for every day.

Love Factor Number 4: You Love WHY You Do It

Now we come to the strongest of the four categories: the why. Or, if you stay with me a little longer, one's personal New York in life. One of my guiding principles is, "If the WHY is strong enough, then the HOW and WHAT will follow on their own." I've already confessed to you that there are many parts of my job that I don't really enjoy. But I love my why. I love helping people lead a self-determined life of personal freedom. I love to make a difference in my readers' lives through my books. I love helping companies take advantage of opportunities for change and establish an appropriate change culture. I love encouraging entrepreneurs around the globe to dream big and act courageously. And most of all, I love to fight my personal battle against indifference and negativity in our society every single day. Because that's the case, I don't need to worry at all about my passion for the HOW and WHAT. They happen almost by themselves. So now I want to ask you the all-important question:

What is your why?

The answer to this has the potential to positively change not only your life, but that of many others, as well.

Whatever your main motivation is, do your job with the utmost passion. A love for your job not only ensures a high inner motivation, but also the essential positive obsession, which in turn is the basis for high quality, excellent results, and thus, enthusiastic customers. Who knows, the next time you're faced with a monotonous or boring task, you might hear a familiar tune inside your head, along with the distinctive voice of John Lennon: "All you need is love. Love is all you need!" Although it's only eight o'clock in the morning as I write this (I'm a morning person and am most productive between six and nine o'clock), I metaphorically raise my coffee cup and drink to my great father, who prepared me in my younger years with this message and started me on my path. Thank you, Dad; I still carry it in my heart today.

NON-NEGOTIABLE CORE PRINCIPLES

Probably the oldest saying regarding change goes, "Love it. Change it. Or leave it." For me, this triad hits the nail on the head in its simplicity. In all areas of life, we have exactly these three options. If we love the status quo, then of course this is the perfect case, because we are intrinsically motivated and enthusiastic to go to work. It gets trickier when we are dissatisfied with any things, conditions, or situations. Then we basically have two options: we can change the unsuitable state of affairs, or—if this isn't possible for some reason—at least change our attitude toward it. For example, we can use a new perspective, gather new information, or increase our choices. And then there is the rare, but definitely possible, case that all our efforts will fizzle out with no results.

In these cases, we have only option number three: to leave the current status quo and navigate ourselves toward new shores.

So far, so good. But what sounds so simple is a great challenge for many people because they don't have the necessary internal compass to guide them to choose one of the three options. This is precisely where the non-negotiable basic principles come into play. It's a concept that I have been using for many years as my personal signpost to help me make important decisions and that gives me the necessary guidance. These principles are the prerequisites, necessary conditions, or requirements that determine whether or not to do things. Let's take my business strategy as a concrete example. When I first wrestled with the concept of non-negotiable core principles many years ago, I asked myself the following question: "What absolutely must be given to make a job permanent, to run a business, or to take a business opportunity?"
What resulted are my four non-negotiable core principles (NCP for short).

NCP 1: I Must Be Able to Act on My Own

Self-determination is my most important value and, therefore, not negotiable. Whatever I do, I must have maximum freedom in my thinking, decisions, and actions. By this, I don't mean that I can do what I want, but that I do not have to do what I do not want to do. It's a small but very decisive difference that is often overlooked. Here's an example. For me today, it's the greatest freedom ever to be able to reject a lucrative offer because the potential customer contradicts all of my values.

NCP 2: It Must Have a Purpose

Life is too short to waste it with insignificance, and I have no desire for purposeless tasks anymore. For this reason, it's also important for me that my work has a meaning. The greater this is, the happier I am.

NCP 3: I Have to Be Able to Earn Money with It

No, not because I'm so keen on having a lot of cash (although I really enjoy making money, even a lot of it), but to feed my family and give my two daughters the best possible future. If I can't earn money with an idea, it may be a nice hobby, but to count as a business, there needs to be a demand that corresponds to the supply. Incidentally, this is one of the main reasons why aspiring entrepreneurs fail. They are so driven by their passion that they forget about important economic principles.

NCP 4: It Must Be Pretty Damn Fun

The world is full of humorless people who manage to spoil every moment with their grumpy attitude. By the way, the German language is the only one known to me in which there is a saying such as "Now all fun aside!" meaning, "You can have your fun somewhere else." I, personally, would like to have as much fun as possible. Not only do I always enjoy an endorphin rush, I also know that you make the best decisions under positive conditions. Not to mention that all the successful people I know have one trait in common: a sense of humor. Because those who can laugh about themselves and their problems can also deal much better with the various challenges of life.

Use your non-negotiable basic principles as personal guides in your life and work.

These are the four most important factors that are crucial to everything I do. They are non-negotiable and serve as a kind of internal constitution for my entrepreneurial existence, and indeed for my life, in general.

I'm well aware that one or more of these values can't be met in the short term. That's okay, because your life is not always a jukebox. In the medium and long term, however, I am not ready to make lazy compromises. If I find that even one of these non-negotiable basic principles is consistently violated, then I take appropriate measures. And now the circle closes, because at this point, we're back to the good old "Love it. Change it. Or leave it."

I'm sure you've been thinking about your own values while reading my four principles, but I'd like to explicitly ask you the pivotal question here:

What are your non-negotiable principles, with which you can pursue your profession with passion and motivation?

Which values are non-negotiable for you and serve as an inner compass for all your decisions in business and in life? The more concretely you can formulate these principles, the more flexible you will be in your behavior. The more you can rely on stable principles, the better you will be able to withstand change, even in times of constant change. Moreover, once you've defined your non-negotiable basic principles, you'll feel an unexpected sense of freedom. For one thing, you gain a wonderful clarity about what you want and what you expect from life. At the same time, you also install an unconscious signal system, which will always sound an alarm if your basic principles are consistently violated. You will then know that it's time to leave. The bottom line is the following rule of thumb:

Stay true to your values and principles, but be as flexible as possible in your behavior.

Or, as Victor Hugo said, "Change your opinions, but stick to your principles. Change your leaves, but keep your roots intact." There's nothing more to add. Grzeskowitz over and out.

Changemaker's Memo: The Five Big Ideas from This Chapter

1. The most important question of your life: What is really important to you?
2. You are not the victim of the universe, you are the universe. Think and act accordingly.
3. Do things with passion, or not at all.
4. Use the power of positive obsession. There are four Love Factors that determine your career success: what you do, how you do it, who you do it for, and why you do it.
5. Formulate your non-negotiable basic principles and you will have a perfect compass for your business and your life.

CHAPTER 3:

External Change through Internal Transformation

Just a small-town girl, living in a lonely world.
She took the midnight train going anywhere.
Just a city boy, born and raised in South Detroit.
He took the midnight train going anywhere.
A singer in a smoky room.
A smell of wine and cheap perfume.
For a smile they can share the night.
It goes on and on and on and on.

—Journey, "Don't Stop Believin' "

A few years ago, I was attending a family party in one of the most famous sports restaurants in Berlin. The proprietor is a local bigwig and has turned an everyday restaurant into something that would be called an "event location" in modern-day terms. Hanging on all the walls are pictures of him with the Who's Who of the German soccer scene, such as Franz Beckenbauer, Jürgen Klinsmann, Lothar Matthäus, Rudi Völler, Waldemar Hartmann, and many others. Just as I was engrossed in these photos at breakfast the morning after the party, a slightly odd-looking man entered the room. He wore a worn-out jogging suit, old-fashioned horn-rimmed glasses, and had two large, full-packed plastic supermarket bags in his hands. He looked rather unkempt and, at first glance, didn't seem very trustworthy.

Out of the corner of my eye, I was able to watch this elderly gentleman go from table to table and try to engage the other guests in conversation, which did not meet with great success. Inevitably, I became a victim of my own prejudices, because the following thought crossed my mind: "Right, so he comes around here scrounging for money." But I was wrong, because things are not always what they seem.

A short time later, the older man came to our table. He had a mischievous smile and said in a friendly voice, "Good morning. Surely you recognize me?!"

I had expected everything but that. It was a classic "Pattern Interrupt," a stylistic device in communication to break (unconscious) patterns.

My attention was aroused, so I answered, "Um, good morning. Please help me a little. How, exactly, do I know you then?"

"Well, through Thomas Gottschalk," replied the man, who had already set aside his two plastic bags.

"I'm sorry, I rarely watch TV, and never watch the *Wetten, dass..?* game show at all. What did you do there?"

The man looked at me, astonished that I never watched the German show that was the basis for the British show, *You Bet!*, and the US show, *Wanna Bet?* "Are you sure? You have to know me. There were two huge articles about me in the *Berlin Morning Post* and in the *Berlin Newspaper*, as well."

"No," I answered. "I'm from Berlin, but I can't remember reading anything about you. What exactly did you do with Gottschalk?"

"Well, I was there for one of the bets. I know every Berlin street and every Berlin subway station. You can happily test me on that. Name any street, and I'll tell you the district and the next largest intersection."

While I was still skeptical, and can't tell you even today if the guy really was on *Wetten, dass...?*, because I was now very curious, I named a road that I knew well. "Okay. Flora Street."

The answer came like a shot from a pistol. "That is found in Berlin's Pankow district. On one end, it leads to Wollank Street and on the other, to Berliner Street. There you will also find the Pankow S- and U-Bahn station."

I was stunned and named another street. "French Street."

Again, he didn't have to think twice. "That is a little street in the city center. It crosses French Street and leads to the opera. The closest subway station is also called French Street."

Take responsibility for your life—and your success.

I was fascinated, because this man actually knew all the streets of Berlin. The small ones, as well as the big ones. The famous and the insignificant. So it happened that we chatted for twenty minutes, during which he recounted his many memories with great passion. And then, just before he wanted to leave, he asked me if I could help him out with a small donation, because he was just a bit short on cash. Surprised, I asked him, "But how can that be, when you have such a unique talent?"

His answer summed it up in a tragic way. "What should I do? Nobody ever offered me a suitable job."

I gave the friendly gentleman ten euros, and then he moved on to the next table. Nevertheless, I had to think about this encounter for a long time. This man is undoubtedly blessed with a great gift that many people probably admire a lot. His memory is capable of things that 99 percent of the population can only dream of. And yet, on this Sunday morning in Berlin, with an old jogging suit and two supermarket bags, he had to go around begging the guests of a restaurant for money because he did not actively use his wonderful talent, but, in a fatalistic way, hoped that other people—or an invisible external force—would ensure the improvement of his situation. What a mistake. And that brings us to another important phrase in this book:

"If you don't take care of your own luck, your success, and your satisfaction, nobody will!"

Yes, success in life is always the top priority. You can let yourself be guided by the expectations of others, make yourself cozy in your comfort zone, and react passively to external circumstances. Or you can assume responsibility and actively shape the desired or necessary change. I'd like to ask you a question that will have a dramatic impact on your future: are you a dodo or a wolf?

OF DODOS AND WOLVES

What, you've never heard of a dodo?[8] It's no wonder, because this (admittedly, not very pretty) bird has been extinct since the year 1681. Since then, it's been considered the prime example of a lack of adaptability. The species perished because they made themselves too cozy in their tranquil comfort zone. It didn't even take one hundred years for the entire species to become extinct. They disappeared one after another.

The dodo lived a happy and carefree life on the island of Mauritius. The dodo was about a meter tall and weighed up to fifty pounds, with blue-gray plumage and a beak more than eight inches long. Instead of a tail, a white tuft of ruffled feathers graced its hindquarters. And, as if such an appearance had not been punishment enough, its wings were so stunted that the dodo was unable to fly. But that didn't matter, because dodos didn't have a single natural enemy. The conditions were paradisiacal in all respects. There was enough living space, more than enough food, and a pleasant climate, which gradually became even more cozy and comfortable, until the day the first humans reached the idyllic island in the Indian Ocean with their boats.

The dodos were so trusting that they didn't perceive any danger at all. And what could be easier for a starving sailor than to kill some birds that couldn't flee, and which even unquestioningly approached humans? But even here, the dodo had a bit of luck in its misfortune—the sailors did not like the taste of its tough meat at all. What ultimately killed the species were the rats, pigs, cats, and monkeys that traveled with the humans. For them, the dodo eggs were particularly easy prey, as they were laid on the ground, basically defenseless. This was the beginning of a swift end. Because of their comfortable living conditions, the pitiful birds had "unlearned" any escape- or defense-related behaviors. And in 1681, their time was up. According to legend, the very last dodo was killed by a Spanish sailor.

Now you may be asking yourself, "It's a sad story, Ilja, but what does it have to do with me?" Very simple. The dodo didn't become extinct because it wasn't very intelligent. Quite the opposite. It was a victim of its own comfort zone, because it wasn't prepared in time for massively changing circumstances. Let's take a look at the facts, because the dodo embodies the classic qualities that are the death of all growth and any further development.

- *Comfort*: The dodo grew up in paradisiacal living conditions, without the slightest need to fear enemies or other external dangers.
- *More of the same, instead of new approaches*: Its comfort zone had been expanded so easily over the years that the ability to flexibly change its behavior had been completely forgotten.
- *Maintaining the status quo*: The dodo species wasted its chances and opportunities to search outside of its comfort zone.
- *Lack of critical thinking*: The dodo was so trusting that it couldn't distinguish between friends and enemies. Instead of taking the future into its own hands—sorry, I mean its stunted wings—it assumed that everything would just continue on the same as it always had been before.
- *Lack of motivation*: The dodo became comfortable, sluggish, and lost all urge to actively shape its own future.

The counterpart to the dodo is the wolf—it has numerous characteristics that are relevant to change.

The entire dodo species assumed that it would continue living *la dolce vita* in Mauritius. Potential changes were not expected, anticipated, or recognized. And we're now back in the midst of our subject, because there are some striking similarities to us humans: entire companies, industries, and societies behave in almost the exact same way. The one difference: the dodos didn't know any better. We humans do—or at least we should—know better, and yet we often ignore the signs of the times.

Let's now look at the counterpart to the dodo: the wolf. This predator, known in Latin as *Canis lupus*, has not only been a great fascination to humans for centuries—presumably because of its strong similarity to the German Shepherd—but it's an absolutely prime example of future-oriented adaptability. For, although the past centuries of growing industrialization and systematic persecution have increasingly limited the natural habitat of wolves, they have managed to adapt to the changing conditions. We humans can learn a lot from the wolf, because its multitude of change-relevant characteristics are captivating:

- *Awareness*: The wolf shines in this area. He senses other animals up to 295 yards away just from the wind, he can hear sounds up to forty kHz (humans hear only up to twenty kHz, by the way), and he can hear other wolves howling up to six miles away.
- *Flexibility*: Due to its high adaptability, there are wolves in a variety of climate zones, including Europe, North America, Asia, Canada, Siberia, and Mongolia. They live in forests, the Arctic tundra, in deserts, wetlands, and even in mountains up to 1.5 miles in altitude. Wolves are swift on their feet, but are also great swimmers. They adapt their hunting and nutritional habits depending on the habitat.
- *Speed*: In times of change, it's not always the best that wins, but often the fastest. The wolf can reach top speeds of up to thirty-one miles per hour.
- *Team spirit:* No one wins alone. Wolves know this, and that's why they show a strong social and territorial behavior. And even though—or precisely because—the individual packs are strongly hierarchical, they attach particular importance to the protection of the weak.
- *View of opportunities*: Whoever wants to take advantage of opportunities in the future has to first recognize them. Not only does the wolf have extremely good night vision, but also a range of vision of 250 degrees. Again, for comparison, a human being has a range of vision of 180 degrees.
- *Persistence*: The wolf has extremely good endurance, and rambles of up to sixty-two miles per night are not uncommon.

Yes, when it comes to active change, we can learn a lot from the wolf. But what about you, dear reader? Do you already use the above-mentioned characteristics in your everyday life? If not, then it's about time you did, because the next few years will be impacted by those who play an active part in shaping them. The future will belong to the wolves, while the dodos will perish due to their comfortable passivity. And yet I have a feeling that in important positions in our society, our companies, and organizations, there are far too many dodos who prefer to wait, hesitate, and blame external circumstances instead of taking life by the horns. With an eye on the increasingly complex circumstances, I'd like to ask you the initial question one more time:

"Are you a dodo or a wolf?"

The answer to this question will determine your future destiny. Because, when it comes down to it, our identity and self-image are always responsible for the results we achieve on a daily basis. Let's take a closer look at why that is the case.

THE CHANGE DIAMOND

We now find ourselves at a critical point in this book. I want to introduce you to the model that has dramatically changed my life. It explains, in a unique way, why some people seem to always succeed in making changes without much effort, while others fail at even the slightest challenge. It's based on the idea of change levels developed by social scientist Gregory Bateson and therapist Robert Dilts. Over the years, I've continued to work to refine, complement, and expand upon this model. The result is my Change Diamond, which can also make a decisive difference for you, if you want to use your personality as the most important success factor for your future. This figure shows an overview of the change model:

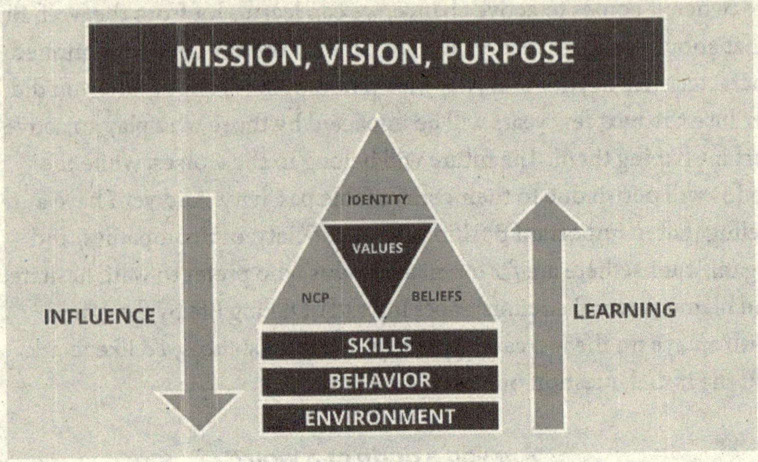

The Change Diamond Model

The idea behind the model can be quickly explained. There are different levels at which changes can be brought about and influence each other. The upper three levels are closely linked, and the central element is Identity, which has a diamond shape. We'll soon see why this icon fits perfectly. But first, let's take a look at each layer.

- *Environment*: Our spatial environment, the people we interact with, and all other external conditions.
- *Behavior*: Our concrete actions, which refers to everything we do, make, and implement.
- *Skills*: The sum of our knowledge, our abilities, and our experiences, which then lead to inner processes, strategies, and programs.
- *Beliefs*: That which we deeply and firmly believe is true. Beliefs act on a subconscious level, always come from the outside, and increase over time. They can be both beneficial and limiting.[9]
- *Values*: The moral principles of our being and the compass of our actions, so to speak. Values increasingly emerge in the course of a life and act on a subconscious level. There are so-called motivation values (drawn to) and aversion values (away from).[10]
- *Identity*: Imagine throwing all your knowledge, skills, talents, experiences, dreams, values, beliefs, strengths, weaknesses, and all other aspects of your unique personality into a big funnel. Then this great mass goes through a special process and, at the bottom,

out comes just a single drop that contains the concentrate of what makes you an individual. That's your identity.

- *Vision, Mission, and Purpose*: You're already familiar with the terms "Vision" and "Mission" in the context of the core needs. In combination with "Purpose," these provide a meaningful life.

Between the levels of the Change Diamond are connections that you should recognize.

So far, so good. Between the different levels, there's the following correlation: whenever a change occurs on one level, it also automatically results in changes on the levels below. This means that top-down is a "Definite Connection." Bottom-up changes may or may not happen. That's why it's considered an "Optional Connection." For example, changing our Values automatically results in changes to the Skills, Behavior, and Environment levels. If, on the other hand, we change our Behavior, this can lead to a change on the higher levels, but everything can also remain the same. An ellipse with an optional Vision and Mission hovers above the model. These factors give our lives a real purpose, and thus have a direct impact on the change levels below them. Have I confused you a bit? Then let me give you a concrete, if fictitious, example.

Imagine that you are the manager of the largest department store in your city (if you live in a rural area, use the nearest city for this little experiment). Your biggest problem child is Mr. Bundy, who is the head of the women's shoe department. On the outside, he is a hard worker, really wants to build a career, and preaches at least once per day about how important change is to him. But on a subconscious level, things look very different. Due to experiences he had when he was younger, he sees himself as a loser and an extremely average salesman. His most important values are selfishness and a fixation on leisure, and his favorite phrase is "Every man for himself." His negative way of communicating often makes him seem like a cynic. He's convinced that customers prefer to be left alone, that selling is hard to learn, and that at fifty, he's too old to be promoted anyway. Although Mr. Bundy doesn't notice these things on a conscious level, this subconscious programming does its reliable service day in and day out—and the results are consistent. His knowledge and sales skills are strictly below average. Every day, a large number of customer complaints come in, departmental sales leave much to be desired, he's often missing, and there's also regular trouble with colleagues.

For you as a boss, it's clear: it's time for a change. You transfer Mr. Bundy to the stationery department. The fashion area was just not right for him, and he's always been interested in office supplies, at least a little. However, there is one problem. His Identity, his Values, and his Beliefs are still the same, and, after an initial sense of accomplishment, his Skills and Behavior remain the same. Despite the new Environment, the results in the stationery department unfortunately have not changed. Here, too, the usual picture: lousy sales, many days off, lots of customer complaints, and trouble with colleagues.

"Okay," you think, "Mr. Bundy is probably just missing the right tools." So you hire a top sales trainer for one week to provide him with all the essential tools: training in leadership, customer approach, handling objections, closing the deal, and add-on sales. However, since Identity, Values, and Beliefs have remained unchanged, this measure does not lead to the desired results.

Of course, you don't give up and suspect that it was probably the sales trainer who simply was not good enough. So you send Mr. Bundy to a sales seminar at a prestigious institute, where he will have the opportunity to work on his skills for five days. Yet here, too, the same thing happens: his Identity as a loser and average salesman doesn't allow any changes at the Skills or Behavior levels. In a last desperate attempt, you have an earnest development talk with Mr. Bundy, in which you give him values and guidelines and tell him, "You just have to believe in yourself." (As a side note, such appeals, with "just" included in the wording, are in principle doomed to failure.) Unfortunately, his unconscious impressions are so strong and stubborn that the results don't change even after this conversation.

Just before you give up, you have a brainstorm. You remember a coaching seminar you once attended in Berlin,[11] and you arrange for Mr. Bundy to get respectful feedback in a nice atmosphere. In this way, for the first time, he becomes aware of his ongoing automatic programming and begins to reflect. He understands that his unconsciously anchored Identity level is standing in the way of his conscious goals, and he begins to work on his personality. And the desired inner transformation suddenly comes. His Identity is changing slowly but surely, and Mr. Bundy sees himself now as a valuable person and a good salesman. This leads to the belief that selling is easy, that customers value good service, and that all doors are open to him when he does his job with enthusiasm and passion. Over time, he forms the appropriate Values, such as customer orientation, team spirit, diligence, and enthusiasm. In order to put all of this into action, Mr. Bundy volunteers to attend seminars at his own expense, regularly reads books, and actively gathers feedback from you as his boss. Due to his new skills and increased knowledge, his Behavior is completely different. He deals professionally with clients, leads his employees with empathy and clarity, closes more sales, and develops many ideas for his department. Well, suddenly the results change, too. Sales rise, customer feedback is extremely positive, and Mr. Bundy is now very popular with employees and colleagues. As a result, he is promoted to the head of the department for the entire first floor and later transferred to the Berlin branch due to his good performance.

The fixed point of the Change Diamond is your Identity.

I hope that this brief example helps you understand why change sometimes works, and often does not. In the Change Diamond Model, there is always a "should" connection from top to bottom, and a "can" connection from the bottom to the top. The most important fixed point is the Identity. It directly interacts with our Values and Beliefs, and it defines our personality, our Behavior, and therefore our results in life. "But wait a moment, Ilja. That would mean that changes at the Environment, Behavior, and Skills levels often don't work?" Exactly. Of course, the regular repetition of a Behavior eventually leads to a change of Identity: we will become what we regularly do. But that is seldom the case. Normally, the Change Diamond will always be the dominant factor.

A good example of this is the series *Goodbye Germany! The Emigrants* which is pretty popular on cable TV. The pattern is almost always the same on it: a dissatisfied and unsuccessful person decides to make a fresh start in Canada or Gran Canaria. So they change their Environment and, usually, their Behavior. But these people forget one important thing—they've brought themselves into this new chosen homeland. Since their Identity and its associated Values and Beliefs remain the same, the results look the same after a short time. The person is frustrated, unsuccessful, and quickly returns from the island they had just chosen as Paradise.

Another example is the smoker, who tries to make a change on the Behavior level by trying to replace the burning sticks with, for instance, nicotine patches, chewing gum, or some other substitute. As long as he doesn't change his Identity ("I'm a smoker") and the associated Beliefs ("It's hard to quit smoking" or "If I quit smoking, I'll inevitably give in"), the success will be short-lived. In the long term, plans like that always lead to a relapse. Only when the Change Diamond is transformed ("I am a happy and satisfied non-smoker") will sustainable results follow.

We can look at it any way we want. If we want to bring about deep and lasting change, then we have to start at the core of our personality. That's why the diamond image fits so well, because our Identity must develop itself over many years. At first, it's often like a piece of coal—gray, dull, and not very attractive on the outside. But through pressure, time, and regular grinding, this once-unimpressive lump turns into the glittering, sparkling, and radiant mineral that has always fascinated people. This leads us to another important saying:

"Every external change always starts with an internal transformation."

Let's take a closer look at how this kind of transformation would work best for you.

TRANSFORMATION, BABY!

"Write a bestseller in thirty hours!", "Get your own expert business in two days. Without any prior knowledge or experience!", or even "You'll never have to work again. Start your online business today and enjoy a monthly passive income of $12,500!" Are you familiar with advertisements like this? When I log into Facebook, I actually run across this kind of marketing every day. The message is always the same, even if the wording varies: "You can succeed overnight without having to do anything!" On the one hand, I'm annoyed by the audacity with which these providers advertise their dubious products and services. At the same time, I'm also a little bit fascinated. After all, enough people must fall for these offers, otherwise there wouldn't be hundreds of ads just like them appearing day in and day out on the internet.

But why is it this way? In the end, the great American performer Eddie Cantor reminded us that it took him more than twenty years to become an overnight success. We all really know that success is always the result of hard work, persistence, discipline, diligence, and sometimes years of setbacks. If only the word *really* wasn't there, because in their deepest core, many people still hope that there is this one secret formula, this unpublished knowledge or magic spell for success, with which one can manage to achieve extraordinary results without any effort.

Unfortunately, this hope is a tragic error. There's an incontrovertible law of the universe that reads as follows:

"You can't get something for nothing."

In order to consume something, it has to first be produced. Financial freedom only comes after saving or investing. A washboard stomach is always the result of a strict diet and a sophisticated sports regimen. And to succeed as an entrepreneur requires a lot of courageous decisions, innovative ideas, and hard work. Without hard work, there can be no success. After all, life is like a staircase; I call this "the Growth Staircase," and I've dedicated the very last section of the book to it. There's also no elevator, and we can't just beam ourselves up. No, if you're really serious about success, you have to climb this staircase step by step. Challenges await us on every single level. We stumble, fail, and make mistakes. But we grow and improve on these steps, until we are finally ready to arrive at the next one. The sequence is always the same:

Action => Make a Mistake => Learn => Grow => Climb to the Next Step of Development

Only when we grow internally and refine ourselves will we achieve the same results externally. Naturally, that means our Identity has to grow at the same time. Only if we can develop our personality can we become a better entrepreneur, boss, employee, salesman, colleague, or manager. There's a question that can help you. Applied regularly, it has the potential to dramatically change your life. I can say that with such certainty because that's exactly what it did for me. I read it in a book once, many years ago, and it has not let go of me ever since. It goes:

How would the person I would like to become behave today?

Even though you might be on the first of ten steps on your personal Growth Staircase, you should imagine now the person you will need to be at the top, and then apply the appropriate mindset, standards, and way of thinking at your current level of development.

Every external change begins with an internal transformation.

When I was Managing Director of the Karstadt department store, I gladly posed the above-mentioned question to my trainees. When I gave them a long lecture on the importance of being diligent, self-reliant, and always having an eye on the team, I received the typical nods of approval, but the information seemed just as typically to be forgotten again—as if by magic—after a few days. However, the small but effective thought experiment connected with the above question went quite differently. No matter what the apprentices dreamed of becoming—whether department heads, personnel managers, or managing directors—the question always had the desired effect. No matter whether these young people were with the company for two days or two years, something changed immediately, because they applied their most important Values, beneficial Beliefs, and especially their desired future Identity to the challenges of the present. In this way, they gradually developed into their envisioned personality.

You can and should make use of this same principle yourself, dear reader, because every external change begins with an internal transformation. No matter which goals, dreams, and visions you have formulated for your future, your Identity must grow into them. Step by step. Depending on where you are today, this may take a lot of effort. You will have to question, make mistakes, and overcome obstacles. At this point, I'd like to quote Arnold Schwarzenegger, whom I greatly admire: "You can't climb the ladder of success with your hands in your pockets." These are the moments that literally shape your character and make you grow and improve until you're ready for the next step. And then the game starts over. Although this path isn't always easy, it's the only one that will lead you to a fulfilled and contented life.

I would like to conclude this chapter with the words of former Czech President Vaclav Havel (who I greatly admire, just because he hired Frank Zappa as a consultant), which perfectly put it in a nutshell: "Vision is not enough, it must be combined with venture. It is not enough to stare up the steps, we must step up the stairs." A wonderful perspective. It's also much more fun if you don't set off as a lone warrior, but surround yourself with like-minded people who support and encourage you. The next part of this book deals with exactly that—the importance of the people you have around you. Would you like for us to climb to the next step together? Then let's go.

Changemaker's Memo:
The Five Big Ideas from This Chapter

1. Take on the characteristics of the wolf in meeting upcoming challenges and discard those of the dodo.
2. The Change Diamond Model explains how successful change works: it operates mainly on the level of Identity, Values, and Beliefs.
3. Your Identity is the linchpin of all your life's outcomes—the good and the bad.
4. Every external change starts with an internal transformation.
5. Ask yourself, "How would the person I want to become behave today?"

PART 2

The People

CHAPTER 4

Nobody Wins Alone

How we all dance with this fire 'cause it's all that we know
And as the spotlight turns toward us, we all try our best to show
We are lost we are freaks, we are crippled, we are weak
We are the heirs, we are the true heirs, to all the world.

—New Model Army, "Ballad of Bodmin Pill"

As a keynote speaker, I have the great pleasure of regularly being invited to exciting conferences and congresses. Since I often speak at the end of these types of events, occasionally I have the opportunity to also listen to the previous speakers. For me, this is pure trend scouting, and, on these occasions, I fill whole notebooks with my thoughts, ideas, and plans. In the last six months alone, I've been able to attend fascinating lectures on artificial intelligence, augmented reality, electromobility, the use of drones, defense against drones, cybercrime, cybersecurity, voice control, and the future of robotics. Although the opinions vary greatly, a common thread runs through the forecasts of all experts: we stand just at the beginning of technical developments that will change our lives. For a long while now, there's been an app for everything, everyday life is managed by our smartphones, and more and more processes are being taken over by artificial intelligence. I am fascinated by what's already possible today, and I feel an almost childlike joy when I think about all the opportunities and possibilities that will arise in the future.

But where there is light, there is always shadow, and for many people, I have the reasonable suspicion that technology doesn't make their life easier, but that they have become slaves to their various machines. They are available twenty-four hours a day, seven days a week, and fifty-two weeks per year, and they check their email every ten minutes—even on family vacations. Haven't you also witnessed a scene in which two people sit together for more than an hour at a cafe and don't talk to each other, but instead they're constantly sending messages via WhatsApp or SMS on their smartphones? Therefore, there is a crucial question for the future: will man's importance be displaced by machines? My forecast is—by no means! We will live in a world that is made easier—but not dominated—by technology and machines. What do I mean by this? Not that digital advances are not progressing as quickly as before. Quite the opposite. I expect even more of this rapid development. However, the deciding factor that many future experts like to forget is the human being, with our unique skills and potential. In spite of digitization, disruption, and all the technical progress, I claim that people will be of primary importance in the future. Certainly, robots, artificial intelligence, and technical innovations will acutely shake up the way we live, love, and work in the years to come. However, for all the importance of these developments, we are all human beings and long for closeness, exchange, and personal communication. Let me repeat my statement once more:

In a future characterized by digitization, disruption, and technical progress, the human being will be the most important success factor.

This has several implications. The quality of your inner circle will decisively determine how your overall happiness and satisfaction are cultivated. And in the professional environment, your employees, colleagues, and team members are not only the guarantors of excellent quality and outstanding results, they are, above all, the greatest factor of differentiation in the face of ever tougher competition. It all comes back to humanity. And I think that's a really good thing. In the first section of this book, we studied how we as humans tick, what drives us, and how successful change is managed. Let's, therefore, change the perspective—away from personal motivations and toward collective success. Away from hard struggles as a lone warrior, and toward successful teamwork. Away from me and toward we. Would you like to do that? Then let's go. And together, for sure, because, as Brazilian soccer star Pelé said, "The only way to win is as a team!"

THE TEAM IS SACRED

Lapland, Sweden. Ten degrees Fahrenheit. The glistening sun is dazzling, and I feel an unforgettable endorphin rush flowing through my body. In front of me, eight beautiful huskies pull my sled, which glides weightlessly through the majestic tundra. What fascinates me even more than the breathtaking landscape is the cooperation of the sled dogs. While there is a very clear hierarchy in the pack, every single husky knows that they can only succeed together as a team. Each animal brings its individual strengths, learns from its teammates, and unconditionally jumps into the gap if one of the others has a moment of weakness. We humans can mimic much of that, especially the powerful energy that arises when individual personalities each assume their place of responsibility, but cooperate at the same time, working together and supporting each other.

If I've learned one thing in the last few years, it's the power of a motivated, competent, and reliable team. As much as I believe in the importance of the individual, without the right people around us, we are all only half as successful. It doesn't matter how good you are or I am, you should never forget the following sentence and should display it prominently over your desk:

Nobody wins alone!

Nobody, absolutely no one, is able to continually succeed as a lone warrior. If, on the other hand, the right people are on our team, we learn from each other, grow together, and support each other. Just so we understand each other here: it's far from being "a team" just because you're sharing an office, working on a joint project, or working in the same company. You may be familiar with the saying "There is no I in 'team' " or that "TEAM stands for: Together Everyone Achieves More." These statements are on the right track. A team is more than the sum of the individual parts. In a real team, everyone is unconditionally there for the other team members, because they have committed themselves to a common vision, and at the same time, everyone takes responsibility in their individual place.

Only a team gives ordinary people the opportunity to achieve extraordinary results. Therefore, the team is sacred.

Even the supposed superstars are completely lost without their team. The British Formula One racing driver Lewis Hamilton needs his mechanic team like he needs air to breathe. Professional soccer player Cristiano Ronaldo can shine only because Sergio Ramos and his defensive colleagues have his back. The great Richard Branson himself, with more than 260 companies, is so successful only because he places his employees at the center of his endeavors. And they pay him back two and three times over with their dedication, performance, and passion.

Which people do you spend the most time with?

In a nutshell, the people you surround yourself with every day are your biggest collateral and, as it were, your greatest success factor on your way to a future characterized by change and insecurity. The team is sacred, both in business and in life. It's your friends, colleagues, business partners, and family members. Because as an individual, you can only grow, succeed, and lead a self-determined life when you are in an environment of mutual learning, appreciation, and trust. Incidentally, the exact same applies to companies.

I cannot emphasize this point enough. In the age of digitization and the global networking that goes with it, the number-one success factor, by far, is the quality of your inner circle, those people with whom you have regular and intensive contact. And that's exactly why the good old quote from the legendary speaker Jim Rohn still stands today:

> ***"You are the average of the five people you spend the most time with."***

This applies on a large scale, but also on a small scale, because we adopt the strategies, attitudes, and thought patterns of the most important people we relate with, as well as their favorite words and habits. In concrete terms, the people you surround yourself with simply make a huge difference, whether your best friends are frustrated cynics watching

TV at home on the couch all day, pulling each other down in a spiral of negativity, indifference, and mediocrity (let me make myself clear here—similarities to real, existing persons are purely coincidental and unintentional)—or if you surround yourself with successful people who create productive value for society, infecting their fellow human beings with positivity, passion, and visionary thinking.

No matter what your specific goals are, surround yourself with people who are already there, where you want to go. I like to use the old slogan, "If you are the smartest person in the room, then look for a new room." I'd go one step further with that, because I've found that there are always two categories of people. The first group are those who want to slow you down, talk you out of your dreams, and for whom you can never do anything right. From these folks, you hear phrases such as, "Just forget about it," "Let it stay the way it is," or "That might work for others, but not for you." They typically give you some kind of reason, such as, "You're too old, too young, too fat, too thin, too tall, too short, too poor, too inexperienced, too loud, too colorful, too different," or whatever. I would therefore like you to never forget this phrase:

You are always too something to somebody.

The sooner you understand that you will never be able to please everyone, and that there will always be people who are looking for a dark cloud even in the sunniest sky and whose acquaintance you should avoid, the more conducive this will be for your personal well-being. So ignore the sourpusses, the whiners, and the know-it-alls, and be sure to focus on the second category instead. These are the people who support you in your personal uniqueness. They accept you just the way you are, with all your strengths and weaknesses. Who also give you critical feedback, but basically support you in all your projects and encourage you unconditionally. Who can butt heads with you, and with whom you can grow—together. In a nutshell: people who just do you good. I myself have used this concept in recent years very consistently—almost radically. Because I know how precious our lifetime is, I only want to spend it with positive, life-affirming, and appreciative people. My inner circle is therefore hand-selected, and I am extremely grateful that I have such great friends, colleagues, and partners by my side.

How is your inner circle selected?

What? Have you never consciously thought about that?[12] Then it's about time for you to build a team with whom you can tackle and shape the future together. It's best to start with a careful inventory. Do you mostly surround yourself with positive people who accept you as you are and support you on your way to your goals, dreams, and visions? If your answer is *yes,* then this is greater than great. However, the probability is quite high that you will find in your immediate environment some good examples of the energy vampires I described above—people who are meticulous in their search for the single hair in the tasty soup, who want to prescribe for you how you should live, and who suck your strength, courage, and energy better than a whole swarm of hungry mosquitoes could.

Just as a soccer coach puts his team together before the season as a matter of course—so that the season's goals can be achieved in the best possible way—you should also choose your team and the people in your environment quite consciously. Your motivation, passion, and mindset will thank you. If possible, get rid of the cynics, the know-it-alls, and the energy vampires today. Instead, surround yourself with positive people, cosmopolitans, and Possibility Thinkers who will accept you as you are and support you in achieving your goals. Just so I'm not painting too rosy a picture for you, let me add one thing. This mental hygiene process can be quite painful, because many of the particularly toxic contemporaries have been in our lives for a long time. But firstly, this step is absolutely necessary if you want to lead a happy and contented life, and secondly, there are so many great people out there who would like nothing more than to take their place by your side.

Get rid of the energy vampires and surround yourself with positive, life-affirming, and appreciative people.

But how do you succeed in getting people into your life who fit perfectly into your inner circle? Basically, this happens in two different ways. One way is for you to make that choice very consciously. Who inspires you, is a role model, or is already at the point where you want to go? Look for ways to get in touch with these people, but please never do so with a sense of entitlement. Although successful people usually like to give, they also have little time and even less desire for their brains and hearts to be tapped by strangers. Instead, ask yourself, "What can I do for these people? How can I help them, or how can I support them?"

My American colleague Vinh Giang, a gifted magician and speaker, recently spoke onstage at Influence, the international speakers conference I travel to each year because people from all over the world are part of my inner circle. Giang recounted how, at the beginning of his career, he sought contact with his great role model, Michael Podolinsky. After many unsuccessful emails, messages, and calls, he changed his strategy. He bought two thousand copies of Podolinsky's book and sent him a picture of himself and the huge stack. Would that attract his attention? It sure did. When Vinh started marketing, promoting, and recommending the book, the time had come. Podolinsky got in touch with his "fan," became his mentor, and over time became a very good friend. The decisive factor is the order. First, give without expectation. This creates a relationship that can then grow and even develop into deep friendship. But more about that in a second.

The second way to bring a variety of positive, life-affirming, and appreciative people into your inner circle is through constant personal growth. At each stage of development, your environment will adapt accordingly. You will attract new friends, colleagues, and business associates as old ones say goodbye. And very few will stay with you throughout your life—be especially grateful for these people. This is the way things go, and I am always fascinated by how strongly the inner growth and the external environment correlate. But whether you're actively looking for an inner circle that will support you in your uniqueness and your individual path, or whether this will happen as a result of the development of your personality, I want to make a recommendation to you. Don't just focus your sights on the one-way street from the inside out, and don't simply surround yourself with people who can supposedly be of use to you. Make a difference. Treat those around you appreciatively and carefully. Be there for your friends, colleagues, and business partners. And above all, make these people big. Act as a motivator, and be the light in a rather dark everyday life.

Make other people big, and you will become bigger yourself.

Not only will this attitude attract many exciting personalities into your inner circle, but you'll also experience a dramatic increase in happiness, fulfillment, and contentment. I'd like to conclude this section with the words of the American writer William Arthur Ward, who said, "When we seek to discover the best in others, we somehow bring out the best in ourselves." How true, because nobody wins alone, and success is always the result of a team that passionately follows a shared vision.

PUT YOUR EMPLOYEES FIRST

"Ilja, it's like this—I'm really open to new ideas and would like to tackle multiple goals at once. However, my colleagues are simply resistant to change and always block my suggestions immediately. It's frustrating. What should I do?" No matter if I'm booked by my clients for a keynote, a daily workshop, or an executive coaching, I hear this call for help—which is often marked by great frustration—more often than I like. The size of the organization doesn't matter, because I hear statements like this in small businesses, medium-sized companies, as well as in international corporations—and from people at all levels of the hierarchy. Employees complain about their bosses, bosses about their employees, and colleagues from marketing about sales and administration. The result: a corporate culture characterized by mutual suspicion, blame, and hostility toward innovation. A vicious circle develops, because if people work more against each other than with each other, then this inevitably leads to a lack of willingness to perform, a lack of customer focus, and ultimately to declining sales.

Establish a culture of change that is shared and lived by every single employee in the company.

If a company has to constantly struggle with missing profits, then staff quickly become nervous and try to counteract it accordingly. The scenario usually looks like this: the C-suite, the HR department, or an external consulting agency remembers the old wisdom of management thinker Peter F. Drucker, who is credited with the statement, "culture eats strategy for breakfast." And then it's decided that the corporate DNA is in urgent need of renovation or reorientation. Basically, this focus is also completely correct, because a culture of innovation, openness, and the courage to try new methods beats each and every sophisticated business strategy, without a doubt. For one thing is certain: if you are good, then your competitors will copy everything. Your products, your prices—maybe even entire marketing ideas. But they will never be able to copy your culture, because this is unique. It's therefore worthwhile to establish a culture of change that is shared and lived by every single employee in the company. In this way, dealing with change will not be a necessary evil, but a natural attitude that will positively impact your sales, customer satisfaction, and profitability at the end of the day.

Yes, it's always the people who make the difference—in the positive, as well as in the negative. However, the implementation of this knowledge in practice usually looks like setting the development of a modern corporate culture as a top priority, hanging big posters with the new company values on the walls, and rolling out corresponding training measures throughout the organization. And then you train—the behavior toward customers, the internal way of communication, or the changing of one's attitude toward the job. The result is, however, usually sobering, because with a few exceptions—even after a completed rollout of such training measures—everything remains the same as it was.

Good common sense tells us very clearly why that is. Motivation, enthusiasm, or passion for one's own profession are all qualities that work from the inside out. They are inseparably linked with our character and our personality. For this reason, they can't be imposed by an external coach or taught through seminars (this should be obvious now, as the Change Diamond sends its greetings from Chapter 3). And so a frustrated and unmotivated employee remains a frustrated and unmotivated employee even after the best behavioral training. As much as we sometimes wish we could, it's simply impossible to change other people. Motivating an existing team and inspiring them for upcoming changes is therefore a difficult, and often expensive, undertaking. It's much easier to pick—right from the start—the most suitable people who identify with your values, goals, and visions for the future. Of course, this presupposes that you're aware of the corporate DNA, your most important values, and your own identity, because only then can you also communicate these formative qualities both internally and externally.

I love the approach of Marriott, the American hotel chain (and one of my dearly valued clients).13 Company leader J. Willard Marriott not only clearly and articulately formulated his aspirations, values, and management philosophy, but also published them on his own homepage. Also, the entire HR strategy of the company is geared toward employing people who can identify with it 100 percent. The results speak for themselves, because in the US, Marriott is known especially for its service-minded and friendly employees, among many other things. When the entrepreneur was asked one day which training methods the company uses to ensure this high standard, he gave a simple but revolutionary response, saying, "We just hire nice people." We just hire friendly people. Why? Because J. Willard Marriott realized that his own team is sacred, so he selects and treats his staff accordingly.

Fortunately, the hotel chain is not an isolated case. More and more companies understand the importance of corporate culture and treat their employees for what they are: the number-one success factor on the path to a future characterized by change and transformation. What may seem a bit exotic at first glance is, on closer inspection, lacking any alternative. To back this up, I'd like to introduce you to a thesis:

In the markets of tomorrow, a focus on employees will be more important than a focus on customers.

Okay, I'm aware that this sentence is most likely the exact opposite of what you've heard, read, and possibly even implemented, because the consensus in business is still that the customer is king. And that's a heavy burden, setting the customer at the focus of all entrepreneurial efforts. After all, with his money, he makes sure that we have something to eat on the table tomorrow and a roof over our heads. Nevertheless, you should always put your employees first. Only then come your customers, business partners, and shareholders. The more clearly you formulate your expectations, values, and demands, the better your team can identify with the corporate culture. This is crucial, because nowadays, a job has to offer more than just a monthly salary and six weeks of vacation each year. Today, people are thirsting for meaning, a deeper sense of purpose, and the feeling that they can make a difference. Always remember: the team is sacred. And that's exactly how you should treat your team. Create a high level of appreciation, an atmosphere in which your employees can grow, and give every single person the opportunity to bring their talents, strengths, and ideas to life.

Create an atmosphere in which your employees can grow and develop.

That last sentence is particularly important, because a good boss is able to inspire a team toward a bigger vision and, at the same time, enable each and every one of them to grow as a human being and realize their own dreams. Yes, of course that means living through change, setting an example, and being ready to give unconditionally. Do you think that's unfair? Perhaps, but what's the alternative? Just take the sun as an example. It puts all its energy into sending out its rays without ever picking one of them up itself. But it gets something much bigger in return: all the plants on the earth turn toward it and follow it. Modern leadership functions the same way. One thing should now be internalized about past leadership styles: the time of traditional bosses is finally over, and I mean the bosses who have led with authority, pressure, and fear.

Nowadays, the highest commandment is to meet each individual person according to their individual needs, to challenge and promote them at the same time. This is how those renowned close-knit teams—who go through thick and thin together and accomplish miracles—emerge. It's nothing more than the natural result of people pursuing a common goal in an appreciative atmosphere and gaining a deep meaning from their personal contribution to it.

At the end of the day, this kind of philosophy leads to the best possible customer focus. Because, if your employees like to come to work with a high level of motivation and a lot of fun, then the satisfaction—and thus, the performance—increases. This ensures that your customers and business partners are treated with a completely different attitude. And all of this is not only true for business, but also for whenever a group of people come together: a sports club, a working group at a university, and of course, for the most important team in the world, the family.

Let yourself be human again. And as radically as possible.

After all, those who understand that personality will be the most important success factor of all will be among the winners in the markets of tomorrow.

WHO WILL CRY WHEN YOU DIE?

Recently, I went to guitar lessons with my daughter Emma. During the short drive through Berlin, she was very quiet and glared out the window. Since she's typically cheerful, I asked her, "What's wrong, honey?"

She answered, "Oh Daddy, I'm not in a very good mood because I have a playdate with Natalie tomorrow."

I was a little surprised and said, "But that's nice, so why are you sad?"

"Because I don't want to. We have nothing in common, and I would much rather play with Maggie."

After this response, I was even more confused and prodded further. "If that's the case, why did you even set up the playdate with Natalie?"

Emma's answer got to the heart of the dilemma. "I just didn't want to hurt her and thought that she would probably be sad if I canceled." At that moment, I was of two minds. On the one hand, I was very proud of my daughter, because she cares so much about the well-being of other people. On the other hand, I also understood that she had subordinated her own needs to Natalie's expectations. She took it upon herself to feel bad rather than do what she really wanted to do.

Are you also familiar with these kind of situations, dear reader? Of course, this example is only about a meeting between two young girls (but still!); however, it also illustrates a pattern that I often observe with my clients: driven by the urge for recognition or the fear of rejection, one lets oneself be guided by the expectations of others, thereby subordinating oneself. To please the boss, colleagues, friends, neighbors, or business associates, you do things you would never choose to do yourself. And then you feel like the plaything of external circumstances, which throw you more or less randomly from side to side. Whether we like it or not, other people affect our well-being more than we would like. And it's not just the stated and hidden expectations. The critics mentioned in the previous section—the know-it-alls or those who use emotional blackmail[14]—also ensure that the behavior of other people will cause us to not feel good. This is because what people around us do, say (or don't say), or expect, simply affects us.

I still remember how a negative email from a former boss once made me brood for a whole weekend. At that time, I was firmly convinced that this could only happen because, through his position in the hierarchy, he had power over me. After all, he was my supervisor, and my professional future was in his hands. Only today, many years later, do I know how wrong I was with this assessment.

It is not other people who have power over us, but we who give them the permission.

By aligning ourselves with their expectations, reacting emotionally to their words, and allowing their behavior to result in us doing things we'd never do ourselves, we initiate a one-sided dependence that will do us no good. To free yourself from this trap, I recommend that you cultivate skills that will greatly increase your personal degree of freedom.

The Art of Saying No

Do you sometimes have trouble saying *no*? Don't worry. You are not alone. On the contrary, my experience tells me that the vast majority basically tend to say *yes*, even though they actually feel, think, or mean *no*. You might be aware of the following examples:

- Your colleague asks you whether you can fill in for her next weekend.
- Your annoying uncle Tony asks if he can celebrate Christmas with you.

- Your customer asks if you can send him the proposal this evening after the end of your workday.
- Your boss asks if you are available to work overtime on an important project.

The more you listen to your internal needs, the greater your success will be in the external world.

Sounds familiar, right? In such cases, many people tend to say *yes*, even though their inner voice screams *no*. To clarify this point, I'd like to give you a concrete example from my own daily activity. A few years ago, I had a coaching client who ran a small but well-run company. The interesting thing was that he achieved just under 80 percent of his sales with only five major customers, for whom he was therefore also available around the clock. It didn't matter how unimportant the request was, he always took care to respond to it immediately. "Wow, what a great service," you may now be saying. Only, the problem was that it was breaking my client down. Constant stress, less and less sleep, and a constant subtle pressure. It couldn't go on like that. At my suggestion that he shut down round-the-clock care—but not the service itself—he responded with a refusal driven by an existential fear. "That's impossible! Then I'll lose my best customers!"

I suggested, "Let's do a test. We'll send an email to your top customers with the following text: 'Dear Customer, As you know, service is very important to us. In order to better meet your individual wishes and needs, we are now available for you from Monday to Friday, from 9:00 a.m. to 5:00 p.m.' Then we'll see what happens. Agreed?"

My coaching client was skeptical, but nevertheless agreed. After four weeks, we saw each other again, and his whole face was radiant. "Ilja," he greeted me with joy, "you won't believe it, but it's going much better than before. Sales have increased, and I finally have time for myself. But the best thing was the mail from my absolute top customer, who wrote and said, 'Of course, your constant availability was very convenient for us, but I've always wondered how you were able to work that way for so long.'"

Why is it that so many people can't say *no*? On the one hand, restrictive dogmas and beliefs often play a role. Here are a few examples:

- If I say *no* now, the other person won't like me anymore.
- If I say *no* now, I'll hurt the other person.
- If I say *no* now, I'll lose my customer.
- If I say *no* now, my boss will think I'm lazy.

And then there is the fear of rejection, dismissal, or possible conflicts. But most often, the reason people say *yes* even though they mean *no* is different: they want to please anyone and everyone. That's precisely where the big dilemma lies. Not only is it completely impossible to please everyone, but this leads directly to a much bigger problem: the more you try to please everyone else, the more you forget your own values, needs, and principles. The consequences are fatal: stress, dissatisfaction, and the gnawing feeling of always being exploited. But it doesn't have to be that way. I even dare to say that the more you listen to your inner needs, the greater your success in the external world will be. You just have to do one thing: learn to say *no* if you don't want something. How does that work? Here are my ten most effective tips for getting better at saying *no*:

The ten most effective tips for getting better at saying NO

1. Accept that you can't please everyone and certainly do not have to.
2. Saying *no* does not mean that you are selfish and can't be there for others.
3. Listen to your values, needs, and principles. They form the basis for every decision.
4. Review your beliefs and replace obstructive beliefs with those that help you to advance.
5. Say *no* if you mean *no*. Clarity creates commitment.
6. Stand in front of a mirror (yes, really do that). Look into your own eyes and then say in a firm voice: "No!"
7. Start with small things and then slowly step it up.
8. Be aware of the reactions to your *no*.
9. The better you know what you want, the easier it is for you to say *no*.
10. In case of doubt, justify your *no*, but never apologize for it.

The more you get used to saying *no*, the better you will feel in your skin, because you are at one with yourself and stand by your non-negotiable basic principles. You'll learn something else, as well. Your reputation will improve with those around you, because you have a point of view and dare to support it. So the bottom line is: if you say *no*, you are also saying *yes* at the same time. *Yes* to more clarity. *Yes* to more accountability. *Yes* to more character.

You Do Not Need Permission from Others

So many people let their daily behavior be guided by others. They do some things to flatter people and refrain from doing other things for fear that people may not like them. But the more one aligns oneself with the expectations and values of others, the more one loses contact with one's own ideas, goals, and priorities. There's one sentence that clearly can't be emphasized enough:

You do not need permission from other people.

You don't need permission from others. No permission to be who you want to be. No permission to do what you want to do. No permission to lead the life you want to lead. Do your thing and enjoy the feeling of self-determination and personal freedom.

The Question of All Questions

Now we come to THE overarching question. It has changed my life very positively and not only helps me to go through life relaxed, serene, and satisfied, but it has also encouraged me to do my thing at all times. I always pose it to myself when I feel that I am driven by other people, thereby moving away from my own needs. Are you familiar with that feeling, too? Someone criticizes you, knows something better, nags, whines, or wants to talk you out of a goal or project? In just such moments, we feel alienated and that we are influenced by both the open and the hidden expectations of these people. The more emotional the relationship, the more strongly this negative emotion works. And who hasn't been annoyed for days by a single comment, a sentence, or even a single word from a person in his own surroundings and let his whole mood be dragged down by it? Sometimes these people even haunt us in our dreams. That time is over, because in these types of situations, the question of all questions comes into play. It helps us to master these situations much more calmly and confidently and to not be influenced by emotional manipulations of any kind. Are you ready for it? Then here it comes, THE question. Whenever you are in conflict with another person, ask yourself:

"If I die one day, would that person stand by my grave and cry for me?"

If the answer is *yes*, then you can count yourself as lucky, because this type of person is very rare. As a rule, these are your family members, friends, or even a very good colleague. These people would walk through the fire for you; their relationship is characterized by mutual trust, esteem, and unconditional loyalty. In these cases, be sure to take the criticism or expectation seriously, and try to arrive at a common solution that everyone can live with based on appreciative communication. With the overwhelming majority, the answer to the above question will be a clear *No*. Please don't give these contemporaries power over you. Every single minute you spend pondering, doubting, or being annoyed is wasted time, because you simply do not matter to these people. Give your negative emotions an opportunity to vent, but then you need to let go of them immediately. Instead, you can put this galvanized energy to better use toward necessary solutions and for the people in your inner circle.

Now it's your turn. Cultivate the art of saying *no*. Disengage yourself from the expectations of others, and ask yourself the question of all questions as often as possible: "Who will cry when you die?" These factors have changed my life decisively for the better. And nothing would fill my heart more with joy, than if it did the same for you, as well.

Changemaker's Memo:
The Five Big Ideas from This Chapter

1. The quality of your inner circle has a profound impact on your results in life.
2. The recipe for success *par excellence*: NWA—Nobody Wins Alone—and the team is sacred.
3. Employee focus comes before customer focus. In this way, you create a corporate culture that makes a difference.
4. Never forget: whatever you're up to, you don't need the permission of other people.
5. Cultivate the art of saying *no*.

CHAPTER 5

The Days of "Harder, Faster, Stronger" Are Over!

I'm coming out of my cage, and I've been doing just fine.
Gotta gotta be down, because I want it all.
It started out with a kiss, how did it end up like this?
It was only a kiss, it was only a kiss,

—The Killers, "Mr. Brightside"

Some of the most famous ads that German commercial television has ever produced emerged in the 1990s. Many Germans remember images of young people biting into Dickmann chocolate kisses straight out of the box. If you wanted to eat light, you resorted to Gervais' Orchard. And my favorite TV character ever—an older woman named Aunt Tilly—praises the benefits of Palmolive dishwashing detergent, into which the young woman sitting opposite her has bathed her hands (why and how she did that will probably remain the secret of the producers forever and ever). My absolute favorite spot comes from 1998 and is set in a restaurant where a yuppie named Schroeder meets with his old school friend Schober. (For the younger readers: a yuppie is a young person who is very successful at work, spends a lot of money on luxury, and lives in a big city.) Following a short exchange of greetings, the showdown between these two peacocks begins. When asked how things are going for him, Schroeder answers, "Brilliant! Wait a moment." Then he reaches into his jacket pocket and places three photos one after the other on the table, while reciting his legendary words, "My house. My car. My boat." Expectantly, he looks his old buddy in the eye. But

Schober's not intimidated and covers the photos on the table with his own pictures, in which much larger status symbols can be seen.

Then he triumphantly says, "My house. My car. My boat," and quickly follows up with three more photos, "My shower (which is pompous). My bathtub (a giant swimming pool). My rocking horse (a beautiful Lipizzaner stallion)."

As the dumbfounded Schroeder, completely intimidated, realizes that Schober is "just like he always was at school," Schober whips out the final blow as, with a smug smile, he chucks a business card on the table and announces, "My investment adviser." The closing slogan of a German banking institution clarifies to the audience how they can also afford a house, a car, and their own boat—"When it comes to money: Sparkasse!"[15]

Yes, I admit that I watched a lot of TV back then, but I'm not reminiscing here because I miss programs like *Married with Children*, *Alf*, *MacGyver*, or *Knight Rider* today. No, when I look back at the Sparkasse commercial, it's only because it was a kind of starting signal for a phenomenon whose affects you can still observe today. I'm talking about the philosophy of "Harder—Faster—Stronger," which will be hereafter referred to as HFS. It's about the pursuit of more and more. More efficiency. More sales. More market share. More power. More prestige. More status symbols. And of course, more recognition from other people. Without a break. Without a deep breath. And without gratitude for what you have already achieved and accomplished.

Life deserves mindfulness, appreciation, and a high degree of gratitude.

For companies, the classic HFS way of thinking is particularly noticeable in the urge to continue to grow the business, not just as far as the KPIs are concerned—the Key Performance Indicators such as sales, productivity, personnel costs, etc.—but also in product development.

You can observe this every day in almost every industry. The cars are getting faster, the skyscrapers higher, and the advertising campaigns more epic. In our personal everyday life, the HFS comes in the form of envy and an extreme focus on external affirmation. The neighbor has purchased a new BMW 3 Series? Then you have to be in a 5 Series. After all, you don't want to be outdone. The frustrating executive position—complete with the eighty-hour week and lack of sleep—is accepted just to prove yourself to your circle of friends. And to be able to show off a flashy Rolex, sometimes a loan is necessary, because of which one then has to work even more. A vicious cycle that is hard to break out of again.

Just so that we understand each other properly, I am a huge fan of achievement, always work at full throttle on the job, and like to reward myself with nice things. I also don't want to give you permission to content yourself with anything less than your true potential. On the contrary, nothing would make me happier than you putting the highest demands on yourself. However, when you commit yourself to the HFS just because you think it's the way to make yourself popular, successful, or important—I have a huge problem with that. Because then you're guided by a definition of success that is not your own, thereby bypassing your innermost needs and values. I always have to think of the old saying by Tyler Durden (brilliantly played by Brad Pitt) from the movie *Fight Club*: "We buy things we don't need with money we don't have to impress people we don't like." There's something to that, right? Because how much is enough? Do you always have to strive for more, or to be harder, faster, stronger, better, or even more efficient? Isn't there a point at which one might be satisfied with one's achievements?

Is it possible for you to be both satisfied and dissatisfied at the same time? Can you be thankful?

Many people are so focused on what they're supposed to be missing, that they completely forget to be grateful for what they already have. And that usually is quite a lot. It's the people in our lives, the work we are allowed to do, and the many little things that we all too often take for granted. I recently read a beautiful story that took place in Egypt more than three thousand years ago. There, the pharaoh—an unsympathetic and bad-tempered guy—in the heat of a hunt, behaved so badly that even his dogs became cranky. They growled loudly, bared their teeth, and chased him toward the Nile, where the next danger was already waiting. Hundreds of crocodiles blocked the king's escape route. They were about to rush on him when the largest reptile of all appeared and offered to transport him safely to the other shore. The ruler was so desperate that he accepted the offer, and to his great surprise, the crocodile even escorted him across the river intact. But on the other side, he realized that it was Sobek[16], the crocodile god, who demanded something in return for saving Pharaoh's life. The pharaoh was to ensure that both he and his people treated the river and all its inhabitants with respect and attentiveness. As long as they were honoring the Nile and the animals, Sobek would ensure the safe passage of their boats. The pact was sealed, and that's exactly what happened. Only once, two thousand years later, did a fleet of military boats forget the deal with Sobek. During this crossing the river claimed over a thousand lives.

I don't know about you, dear reader, but in this little fable, I immediately think about us humans and our dealings with each other and with the resources of this earth. Even if we don't encounter any crocodile gods in our everyday life, life will take its toll if we don't honor it with mindfulness, appreciation, and a high degree of gratitude. For this very reason, I think the time is overdue to put an end to the reign of "Harder, Faster, Stronger." To plead for less, and at the same time more:

- Less superficiality.
- Less egotism.
- Less perfection.
- Less indifference.
- Less envy.
- Less optimization mania.
- Less restlessness.

And therefore:

- More depth.
- More mindfulness.

- More meaning.
- More responsibility.
- More purpose.
- More appreciation.
- And more gratitude.

Anyone who, like a poor donkey, constantly chases after the carrot of external expectations is moving away from their innermost core. And that—sooner or later—leads to dissatisfaction, frustration, and burnout.

Instead, I campaign for maximum gratitude, a personal definition of satisfaction, and an exclusive focus on your own expectations, goals, and needs.

What do I mean by that? If your personal definition of success is the accumulation of material wealth, steep advancement up the career ladder, or an exclusive focus on maximizing profits, then you may be part of the small minority for whom HFS is exactly the way to go. If, on the other hand, you have different priorities, such as the compatibility of family and work, the placement of value on purpose and meaning, or you want to give something back to society with your company, then you should urgently adjust your course. That's precisely what we're aiming at in this chapter. We're looking at how to find a true mission in life, what changing batteries has to do with deep fulfillment, and how to break away from other people's expectations and just do your own thing. The great art is to be satisfied and dissatisfied at the same time. Satisfied with your own life and dissatisfied with the *status quo*. Because only in this way do we feed our inner hunger, which ensures that we grow and really make use of our full potential.

Do you want to know how this balancing act works? Great! Then, let's move ahead. And if you feel any doubt, uncertainty, or pressure to perform during this process, I'd like to share with you the mantra of former football coach, and later insurance giant, Art Williams[17]:

"All you can do is all you can do. But all you can do is enough."

A sentence with real depth, which has been a reliable guidepost for me for many years in the often tough everyday life.

THE ATTACK ON THE DEATH STAR

I'd like to ask you a very direct question: "Who is your greatest enemy?" What? Have you never thought about that? Or, worse yet, you have none? Then you should change this situation as quickly as possible, because if we talk about personal development, then the following applies:

Your greatest enemy is, at the same time, your best friend.

The reason for that is because he drives you emotionally, challenges you, and helps you to grow as a human being. Each hero can develop his superpowers only because he has an equal arch-rival, against which he has to constantly measure himself. Without his overpowering opponent, the dark lord "You-Know-Who" (a.k.a. Voldemort), Harry Potter would just be a short, shy wizard with round glasses. Jedi Knight Luke Skywalker would never have been able to destroy the Death Star (and thus save the galaxy) if he hadn't had a fearsome adversary in Darth Vader. Without his nemesis, Moriarty, even the brilliant master detective Sherlock Holmes would have been just a simple snooper with a badly fitting hat, who would have sat around 221B Baker Street hoping in vain for assignments.

Truly, every great hero has an enemy against whom he measures himself and from whom he draws all his strength. Would you like a few more examples? Frodo Baggins battles against Sauron, Scrooge McDuck has Flintheart Glomgold, Indiana Jones has the Nazis, Batman has the Joker, starship *USS Enterprise*'s Captain Picard has the Borg, Gru's archvillain is El Macho, and Rocky's Apollo Creed. Let me ask the original question again: "Who is your greatest enemy?" I already hear your objection: "Come on, Ilja, I'm just a normal entrepreneur. My life is nothing like in the movies. Why would I have an enemy?" I agree, of course, and I don't want to incite you to mess with your biggest competitor on a personal level. But in business, too, all successful brands have their big rivals they compete against. Apple with Microsoft, Adidas with Nike, Proctor & Gamble with Unilever, Bank of America with Wells Fargo, Coca-Cola with Pepsi, Mercedes with BMW, Fender with Gibson, Sony with Canon, TaylorMade with Callaway, Rolex with IWC, Marlboro with Camel, Walmart with Target, New York Yankees with Boston Red Sox, or Hilton with Marriott.

Do you see what I'm getting at? Only through their particular enemies are these heroes, brands, or companies able to bring forth their best possible performance—primarily because the duel is not just about numbers, dates, and facts, but is driven by emotions, feelings, and unconscious factors. And now comes the interesting bit. An enemy doesn't always have to be a villain, a rival, or a competitor. The most powerful motivation springs from the fight for, or against, something higher. Against oppression, violence, or poverty. For justice, freedom, or women's rights. Whoever knows what he's fighting for, what he's come for, and what his mission in life is, is also ready to give it their all. To cross over the boundaries. And to always invest a little bit more than is actually necessary. Because it creates an inner drive that gives their own work, company, or job a deeper meaning; and for something that has meaning, you're always ready to relegate everything else.

Let me phrase the question a little differently then:

What do you stand up for and which larger thing are you fighting against?

Is it mediocrity, selfishness in this world, or something completely different? My greatest enemy for many years has been the indifference that I have battled against with heart and mind. This state of passivity, lack of thinking, and absence of self-determination that seems to increasingly spread around the world like a virus. So I've decided not to accept this trend any longer. No matter whether I'm writing a book, holding a keynote speech on a big stage, or supporting a medium-sized company in a change process, my mission is always to lead a self-determined life marked by purpose and personal responsibility. To grab the future by the horns and make a difference. That's what I live for, and my whole business is based on this stance. And in this way, my greatest enemy becomes my best friend. Because I know why I do what I do every day. Because my work has a meaning that helps me do the less-than-exciting tasks with a smile on my face. Because I grow beyond myself in the fight against indifference and use my resulting superhero powers to make the world a little better than I found it.

Does your work also have a purpose that helps you do the less-than-exciting tasks with a smile on your face?

I'd like to encourage you, too, to find an enemy to butt heads with. One that often seems overpowering but enables you to grow as a person. One that gives your life, your job, and all of your work a real sense of purpose. And then you align everything with this mission—like what you do, as well as what you do not do anymore. You will fight epic battles and suffer some defeats, too. At the same time, you'll experience an unprecedented fulfillment that automatically sets in whenever you are on a crusade for a greater cause that positively affects the people around you. But before you can destroy the Death Star, throw the ring into the hearth in Mordor, or fight the final duel against Voldemort, it's time to define your own personal mission. Because when it comes to meaning and purpose, your greatest enemy is—at the same time—your best friend. Choose it wisely, because it will dramatically affect the course of your life.

THE WORLD NEEDS MORE BATTERY CHANGERS

It was an ordinary Tuesday afternoon. As happened so often, the entire squad of department heads was sitting in the large meeting room of the department store for the weekly meeting. As the managing director, I used these appointments to inform my department leaders about current topics of interest, to present financial figures, and to plan joint activities. On that day, the individual departments would present their strategies for the upcoming Christmas season. Back then, that time of year made up more than 70 percent of annual sales; things are very different in these modern times of permanent sales and online shopping. Ms. Fletcher (not her real name), from the ladies' outerwear department, started things off. But when she wanted to click the button to present the first PowerPoint slide, it didn't work. Frantically, she clicked on the remote control and stared hopefully at the projection screen. A familiar strategy. I'm sure you've seen people who stand in front of an elevator and hope that—if they just press the button often enough and hard enough—it will come faster. But repeating the same (and ineffective) behavior over and over again has never led to different results. And so it happened that even the tenth click on the remote control did nothing. The start screen was still visible, but the device just didn't work.

It wasn't long before a murmur started in the room and grew louder by the second. "Somebody needs to do something," one person said.

"Typical IT Department. Even they don't get it," someone else said.

A third colleague complained, "With the ancient equipment we have to work with around here, it's no wonder it doesn't work."

Almost all the department heads joined in the moaning and blaming. And the criticism was hurled at everything—the technicians, the administration, the headquarters, the incompetent colleague who couldn't use the technology, me, and even the executive board. The mood was boiling. All because the projector didn't work. It probably would have continued for some time longer, had the young head of the Perfume Department not done something that interrupted the endless spiral of negativity and criticism. She rummaged in her purse, rose from her seat, and wordlessly stepped forward. Then she took the remote control from a bewildered Ms. Fletcher, opened the flap, and changed the batteries. "So," she told her colleagues, "it's working again. Can we continue now?"

Are you one of those people who want to act, make a difference, and take responsibility?

I've thought about this experience a lot lately, because the feeling creeps into my mind that fewer and fewer people are daring to create or follow through. Instead, we've become a society in which the masses happily prefer to consume pre-packaged contents and to let themselves be lulled externally. I noticed this again when I was in Orlando. In addition to my business appointments, I had some time to visit both Universal Studios and Disney World. And, although the 3D rides and roller coasters are loads of fun to me, I've become aware of what's actually happening in these kinds of amusement parks. Every single day, tens of thousands of people are operating in maximum consumption mode and rely on the fact that "the man"—as "the one up there" is popularly called—will provide them with everything they need. With entertainment, fast food, and countless other ways to spend money on trivial stuff. I'll say it again, I don't mind indulging in all the fun and thrills for a day. And yet I can't shake off the fear that this attitude of passively letting life wash over you will become more and more prevalent. Because people have forgotten to think for themselves, to create their own experiences, and to use their imagination to have a good time—just like that and without any external stimulus. I'm not even talking about creating value for your personal environment, your own team, or society.

The few courageous ones who are daring then have to deal with critics who—from a safe distance away, unsolicited—will proffer their opinions, attack below the belt, and basically think they know everything better. Of course, these know-it-alls would never say these things to your face. Instead, they like to hide in the anonymity of the internet—because where else can you give your own frustration free rein and finally say what you always wanted to say? Take a look at any Facebook feed and you'll see what I mean. It seems a little bit like *The Muppet Show*. Do you remember that? The two senior men—Waldorf and Statler—sat up in their cozy balcony and commented on everything, heckled, and tore into what was taking place below them on the stage.

Aren't there exactly these two types of people in real life, as well? There are the ones who act, who get things done, and who take responsibility—the business owners, firefighters, nurses, referees, writers, self-employed, founders, police officers, teachers, mothers, and anyone else like you and me who create, do, and are productive. But whoever acts also, inevitably, makes mistakes. Becomes vulnerable. Offers themselves as a perfect target. Then there are the others—those who are far removed from actual events. Who immediately run for cover when things heat up, when it starts to hurt, when push comes to shove. But, of course, they reserve the right to criticize, judge, and tear into the actions of the people who are acting on the stage of life, in the distance.

Destructive criticism and grumblings are massively annoying!

I'm not talking about constructive criticism here. That type is helpful, not only because of the way it's formulated, but because it's absolutely necessary for change. No, I'm talking about the increased level of anonymous bashing, hurtful slamming, and insubstantial verbal abuse, which sometimes take on absurd forms. But why does that occur? For what reasons do people forget all their manners and treat those around them with so little respect? Is it a lack of self-confidence, envy, or a general dissatisfaction with their own life? I couldn't tell you exactly, though it's probably a mix of all of the above. But I know one thing for sure: it's massively annoying. I've just read two reviews for one of my books on Amazon.[18] Both were one-star reviews that didn't even respond to the content but merely bristled with personal hostility. And, of course, neither of the two "critics" dared to write under his own name. Verbal low blows are much easier on the lips or the keyboard when you're behind the safe mask of a pseudonym.

Naturally, I realize that my opinions, my content, and my personality can be quite polarizing. I'm not interested in pleasing everyone. I also know that exhibiting a clear angle also means saying things to some people who don't want to hear them. Nevertheless, I have a basic problem with these anonymous insults lobbed from the balcony. Why? Because this kind of destructive way of communicating can have fatal consequences. Personally, I have a thick skin in this regard and am well able to withstand that. Although it takes some strength, for me it's also the price I pay for being exposed on the stage. For many other people, however, such a thing can be absolutely life-threatening. Think of the restaurant run by its owner (with words such as "disgusting," "nauseating," and "unacceptable" on the relevant review sites), the small shop around the corner ("terrible service," "rude," "awful"), or the babysitter from the neighboring town ("can't handle children," "gets angry quickly," "unsuitable").

These are just a few examples of many, and I'm sure you could think of many more. As a society, we are now faced with a fundamental decision: are we tolerating this kind of reciprocal interaction, or are we sending a signal? We should never forget one thing:

The tolerance of intolerance has never led to more tolerance.

Therefore, I've decided not to silently accept this alarming development. In the name of all productive and courageous people who are taking action, I would like to call out the know-it-all critics:

> *We appreciate any constructive criticism because we know that we can only continue to evolve, improve, and grow. We can also deal with plain language, harsh arguments, and direct words—when they are communicated openly and appreciatively. Otherwise: be quiet up on your balcony! We simply have no interest in know-it-alls, complainers, and whiners who use us—without our consent—as a projection screen for their own fears. We don't need your negative comments lobbed from a safe distance. We also don't need any insults, instructions, or defeatism. If you want to have a say, then leave the comfort of your balcony and come join us on the stage. Come here, where it hurts. In the heat of the battle. Where blood, sweat, and tears flow. The world doesn't need any more people who think they know exactly what everyone else is doing wrong. Instead, the world desperately needs more people like my junior manager in the Perfume Department. It needs people who act courageously, dare, make mistakes, and create productive value for themselves and for others. Who are mindful in their dealings with themselves, their fellow human beings, and their environment.*

The world needs more battery changers!

The time has come for each of us to make a decision. Do we want to take responsibility or to talk about the achievements of others? Are we productive and go where it hurts, or do we strictly consume and then criticize what actually happens from our comfortable balcony? Do we want to be battery changers or know-it-alls?

We can choose either the right way or the easy way.

One way inevitably leads to a destructive spiral of negativity, frustration, and self-destruction. The other requires a lot of courage, commitment, and stamina, but it's the only way to real happiness and deep fulfillment. Because only those who act proactively, create productive value, and grasp the future by the horns experience the unique feeling that arises when you are in the driver's seat of the bus of life—and not sitting helplessly in the last row watching as others steer toward the abyss at full throttle. We all have the choice, every day! I've made my choice. Which do you choose?

LESSONS IN GRATITUDE

If you've read other books by me, then you'll know that I'm a big fan of Zig Ziglar. There were times when I listened to the complete audio tapes of his brilliant lectures while I was out jogging. Again and again. That's because I've always been fascinated by the supposed ease with which this little man—with his likeable southern slang—makes such a huge difference. As usual, if something looks particularly easy, that means there's a whole lot of work behind it. One of his messages in particular has influenced and shaped me:

"You can have everything in life that you want, if you just help enough other people to get what they want."

It took me a long time to understand the real meaning of this sentence, which I had originally dismissed as the abstract wisdom of a guru. Only today, many years and many experiences later, do I know how right good old Zig was with his statement. Because I've learned one thing since then: there's definitely a very clear order for how success arises. It is: Give. Give. Give. Then, and only then, comes phase two: the receiving.

Success goes like this: Give. Give. Give. Only then comes the receiving.

In recent years, I've had the great honor of meeting many personalities. And the more successful they were, the more they had internalized that particular giver mentality. I've already suggested this in Chapter 4. I don't mean giving with the ulterior motive of getting something in return. On the contrary, I speak of unconditional giving in order to do something good for other people. Simply like that. Because you can. Because you have certain knowledge, contacts, or skills, or you're able to help others to reach a goal more easily.

In Europe, especially, I get the feeling that this philosophy is not very common in practice. Instead, their own ego is put in the foreground, and elbows are ruthlessly used to enforce their own interests. But why is it that way? The reason for this is basic lack-based thinking—the fear that there is not enough for everyone. The worry that someone could take away a piece of the cake—such as the customers, market share, or sales. Do you also know people like this? I have come to consistently avoid these kinds of people and radically banished them from my inner circle. I learned from my American friends who are also speakers that there is another way. Every year, I travel to the world's largest conference of speakers, because I get so inspired by the attitude of mutual serving, sharing, and enrichment. The members of the National Speakers Association—NSA—have absorbed the spirit of their founder, Cavett Robert, with every fiber of their being. Many years ago, he said:

"We never fight over the size of our slice of the pie; we just build a bigger pie."

Isn't that a wonderful philosophy? The nice thing is that it's not just an empty phrase—all NSA members live by it. By the way, the unofficial slogan of the NSA is: we are the ones who speak, not who listen. I've never experienced such unconditional generosity and the need to give something as on my travels in the USA. And it has become a mission of mine to bring the spirit of giving to those in Europe, where I live. For I am deeply and firmly convinced of one thing:

There is enough for everyone. And there is enough of everything.

Nothing would make me happier than if, right now, you would make the decision to join my mission—to create a bigger pie, together—and to let the wind of generosity flow through our selfish egoism. Break yourself free from always thinking about "lack" and surrender instead to abundance. Specifically, this means making other people big, strong, and successful. Help them to get what they dream of. Believe me, nothing is more fulfilling than helping others grow, because you'll experience a deep sense of gratitude. Would you like to test this? Are you stuck with low motivation, have little energy, and are frustrated? Help another person! Just by shifting your focus, your condition will improve. And why is that?

You can't be both grateful and in a negative mood at the same time.

That's what I like to call "Lessons in Gratitude," because that wonderful feeling is the best and most perfect antidote to frustration, negativity, and a bad mood. Would you like a few examples?

You can't be grateful and unmotivated at the same time.

You can't be grateful and dissatisfied at the same time.

You can't be grateful and sad at the same time.

You can't be grateful and angry at the same time.

You can't be grateful and hopeless at the same time.

You can't be grateful and aggressive at the same time.

You can't be grateful and cranky at the same time.

You can't be grateful and frustrated at the same time.

Do you see where I'm going with this? For me, gratitude is the universal key to a fulfilled life. "Ilja, that sounds very simple, but what should I be grateful for?" You don't even know how many things are just waiting to be noticed by you. That's why I say, "Mindfulness, Baby!" Don't you think we take too many circumstances for granted? The people around us, the work we're allowed to do, and of course our health. We should be infinitely grateful for all these things that have been given to us. For what we treat with mindfulness automatically increases in value. And if we pay attention to the small things—the supposedly obvious and inconsequential moments—with a high degree of gratitude, then our lives will be rich, fulfilled, and incredibly beautiful. Try it! I guarantee you that there is nothing more fulfilling than waking up in the morning with a deep sense of gratitude, and going to bed with the same attitude in the evening.

Make other people big, strong, and successful.

But back to the positive effect of the spirit of Cavett—not to fight for a larger piece of a small pie, but to build a bigger pie together. Amazing things happen when you make this attitude a daily habit. Because the more you unconditionally give and make other people great—instead of cheating them, hurting their self-esteem, and making them small—the more you will get in return. Not always from the direction or from the people you would expect, but you'll see how your karma account balances out over time. The more you give, give, give, the more you will receive, receive, receive. The more you integrate the spirit of Cavett Robert into your everyday life, the more Ziglar's mantra will do its service for you. The more you encourage other people and help them to get what they want, the more you will get exactly what you want.

So ask yourself regularly who you make strong, and what you can offer to whom. And not with the intention of getting something back, but simply because you like to give, and because you can. Once you start doing business using this philosophy and supporting the people around you in their growth, the more great things will come back to you from different directions. That is definitely not esoteric wishful thinking, but simply a universal law from experience.

Changemaker's Memo: The Five Big Ideas from This Chapter

1. The times of "Harder, Faster, Stronger" are over. Instead, humanity, meaning, and gratitude are what count.
2. To improve, you need an enemy to butt heads with so you can grow. What's your enemy's name?
3. Every day, we have to make the decision whether we want to be a passive know-it-all up in the balcony, or a battery changer on the stage.
4. There is a clear order for how success arises: Give. Give. Give. Then comes the receiving.
5. The most important lesson in gratitude: you can't be grateful and in a negative mood at the same time.

CHAPTER 6

The Motivation Revolution

She says: We've got to hold on to what we've got.
'Cause it doesn't make a difference if we make it or not.
We've got each other and that's a lot for love—we'll give it a shot.
Woah. We're half way there. Woah-oh. Livin' on a prayer
Take my hand and we'll make it I swear, livin' on a prayer

—Bon Jovi, "Livin on a Prayer"

Some time ago, I received a very nice email from a reader named Mrs. Weber, telling me how much my books had helped her to turn her life upside down when she was almost fifty years old and to do what she had always wanted to do: open a shop for craft supplies. Her comments were so florid that I blushed more and more with each sentence. Until I came to the last paragraph, where she said "But I have one more thing to tell you, Mr. Grzeskowitz. If you had left out all the soccer examples, your books would have been twice as good."

But what should I do? I love soccer, and I also think it's a wonderful metaphor for life in all its facets. Anyway, I only tangentially mention that I'm a fervent fan of Manchester United. Well, dear Mrs. Weber (I have changed the name of the reader), if you are reading this book (which I would very much like you to do), then I suggest that it's best to just get it over with, okay? Actually, I would like to take you on a short journey into the past. Back to a time that, for me, was four of the craziest weeks that I have experienced since I have been living in Berlin. We're writing 2006 as the year, Germany is hosting the World Cup in soccer, and I am managing director at Karstadt in Berlin's Tempelhof district. The city is a colorful melting pot of people from all continents, celebrating together, watching soccer, and just having a good time.

My personal highlight of this summer fairy tale took place on June 30, when I was invited by a customer to the quarterfinals of Germany against Argentina. No, unfortunately not in the Olympic Stadium, but in the Sony Center on Potsdamer Platz, where we watched our boys on the big screen together from box seats in a balcony and shared in the excitement. The mood was just outstanding, and rarely have I experienced such a positive euphoria as I did then. To top it all off, our national team—which back then was not responding to their artificially branded name, "The Crew" (not everything that's new is also better)—won four to two in a dramatic penalty shoot-out. In particular, the note that goalkeeper Jens Lehmann was slipped from his biggest rival, Oliver Kahn, was the big topic of conversation of the assembled journalists.

We are responsible for our own motivation.

Even though the game was filled with emotions, hustle, and exuberant passion, the real goosebumps came afterwards. During the entire World Cup, director Sönke Wortmann accompanied the German national team with his camera, and he compiled the best scenes in his film, *Germany: A Summer Fairy Tale*. One of the highlights of this documentary is undoubtedly the speech by the coach, Jürgen Klinsmann, before the above-mentioned game against the players from Argentina. Do you remember that? We find ourselves right inside the German team's locker room. The players sit on their benches, deep in concentration. You can almost feel the tension in the air. Jürgen Klinsmann stands in the middle with his sleeves rolled up, and he speaks the legendary words in his Swabian dialect:

> *They're scared stiff, they're scared stiff. They come here with a defensive lineup, they're shitting their pants [...] We are always on the move, we're always there. We're always cheek to jowl. It's about to bite. Controlled, highly aggressive, but disciplined. That's why we have our captain...they haven't met our captain yet. Twice, we had them on the ropes, (again, louder) twice, we had them on the ropes.*

> *Without Micha [Michael Ballack]. But today they're in for it. I swear to you, guys. They're in for it. They are really in for it, okay?*[19]

Then a collective battle cry sounds through the cabin, and the rest—as they say—is history. That brings me to the very reason why I'm telling you all of this. This legendary speech by the national team's coach caused a greater jolt to go through the nation than a similar speech by former German President Roman Herzog had done. After many years as Sleeping Beauties, people suddenly became intensively interested in the subject of motivation, which found its way into the most diverse areas of life within a very short time. No wonder. If Bastian Schweinsteiger, Lukas Podolski, and Philip Lahm could grow beyond their former selves by having the right inner drive, then this would have to be possible for John Doe.

A whole country longed to bring the euphoria, positivity, and energy of the Summer Fairy Tale into everyday life. Of course, it didn't take long for companies to increasingly focus on motivational trainers who could push the various teams in sales, marketing, or purchasing to new heights. However, the more people concerned themselves with motivation, the more they realized that the methods of the past would no longer be sufficient for the challenges of the future. This is even more true today. Just look at the evolution of the last ten years. In this period, more has changed than in the hundred years before that. Whether in society, the economy, or our private environment, nothing is as it once was, and the pace of the (sometimes serious) changes is increasing rapidly. We can twist it and turn it the way we want to:

The better we are able to motivate ourselves, the better prepared we will be for the challenges of the future.

Motivation Is a Top Priority!

Yes, you read that right. Of course, motivation is a top priority, and every single day we must think about why we do what we do. Well, that's not always easy, because we regularly have doubts, struggle with problems, and think about throwing in the towel. Therefore, it's so incredibly important to give ourselves a loving, but firm, kick in the butt again and again. Because if you don't, then no one will. No one knocks on your door in the morning and presents you the opportunity of your life on a silver platter. No fairy appears out of thin air to make your innermost wishes come true by magic. And Jürgen Klinsmann—or more contemporary successful soccer coaches, like Jose Mourinho, Pep Guardiola, or Jürgen Klopp—won't appear in your office if you need a little motivation on a tough day. So I'm sorry to say at the end of the day, you are fully responsible for your motivation and your choices—and, therefore, for your results. Unfortunately, this realization is still in gross contradiction to the conventional approach of motivational theory. But there's also good news. You already carry within yourself everything you need to sustainably—and with a great deal of inner drive—change. You just have to discover it, bring it to the surface, and apply it daily.

We are in the midst of the journey between being an information-driven society to being a purpose-driven society.

Together with you, dear reader, I'd therefore like to usher in a paradigm shift. Even though the future will be shaped by technological developments such as artificial intelligence, robots, and automation, it will always be intrinsically motivated people who use the technology and actively shape the future with the many new opportunities. Why can I claim this so vehemently? Because we are in the midst of the journey between being an information-driven society to being a purpose-driven society. Just a few years ago, data, information, and knowledge were the key assets. Today, the key assets are a deep sense of purpose, living according to your individual personality, and the compatibility of your job and your life. Of course, this also means that our personal approach to motivation must adapt to these changed conditions. A new, modern approach is necessary to meet the needs, values, and demands of the twenty-first century. The motto is: kick your own ass!

Kick your own ass, instead of waiting for others to motivate you.

When we pursue our goals full of passion, enthusiasm, and dedication, we also instill these strong emotions in other people. To flip the rusty switch, it is essential that the term "motivation" finally shakes off the dubious, shoddy image of its past. I don't know about you, but I think that's overdue. The world is in one of the biggest transformation processes of the last 250 years. The old chimneys and steam engines of the past are the completely wrong tools for the challenges of the future. The era of *Tschakka*-bellowing motivational coaches, of esoteric gurus preaching light and love, and the blunt use of carrots and sticks is simply over.

The era of Tschakka Tschakka is over!

From day to day, people increasingly feel that there are no more prizes to be won with hollow phrases and false promises. Instead, they crave purpose, values, and sustainability. Yet personal development, growth, and change are still being sold and taught today—as was the case in Helmut Kohl's time, shortly after the fall of the Berlin Wall. Go to any motivational seminar of your choice and you will find the same patterns. A determined "Becker Fist" here, a fervent wish to the universe there, and a cornucopia of metaphors that are so exhausted that one would like to sink into the ground from shame while listening. The results correspond. In the short term, the recipients of these insubstantial motivational shots are also full of energy and feel like they can pull all of the trees out of the earth at once. But a crash back into the familiar listlessness follows this steep rise as certainly as day follows night. One flees into cynicism, indifference, and sarcasm.

It is precisely this superficial approach that has ensured that the term "motivation" is perceived negatively these days and is why the motivational coach's job has an equally bad reputation. If only it were a real profession: many self-proclaimed motivational trainers have gone to merely one weekend seminar and feel called to carry their messages into the world. Because I know the incredible power that can develop from a motivation born of purpose and reason, this development makes me angry. At the same time, I wonder why so many people still fall for the false promises of the supposed prophets. After many years of observing, researching, and thinking, today I'm sure that the answer lies in a simple—but fatal—truth:

And most motivational phrases are so wonderfully packed in frills that you just want to believe them. Deep inside, we feel that something is wrong. But the alternative is that we have to make difficult decisions, work hard, and we really have to change. Since most people aren't ready for that, as in the good old Matrix, they swallow the blue pill and put their faith in the false promises of the motivational gurus.[20]

Would you like a few examples? Here we go:[21]

- You can do anything.
- You just have to want it, the rest will follow on its own.
- The universe will take care of your success.
- Everything is fine the way it is.
- Strike the word "impossible" from your vocabulary.
- Whatever's supposed to happen, will happen.
- If you can't reach a goal, then it wasn't meant to be.
- From now on, we don't say there's a problem, but a great opportunity. (This sentence is my absolute favorite. Anyone who says that has never had real problems.)
- You must tell the universe what you want, then it will manifest in your life.
- You just have to look at it positively.

Do you understand what I mean? Although there is a small spark of truth in all these sentences, these slogans are tempting you to take the easy path, instead of investing the necessary work. You scratch the surface a little, instead of getting to the core of what drives you. Instead of using your heart and mind alike, suddenly everything is just a mental block, playing around inside your head, or not working at all because Mercury is in retrograde. (I admit it, I always wanted to write this sentence in a book ☺.) These motivational phrases are usually rounded off with a firm knock on one's own chest, a hopeful look toward the universe, and finally, a convincing, "Tschakka, you can do anything!" Then, if you crash and fail, you're left wondering why. Incidentally, I will not go into more detail about the currently very popular glorification of the subject of "failure" at this point, otherwise I would be opening another Pandora's box.

It breaks my heart again and again when I meet people who want nothing more than to make a change, and then experience a crushing failure due to the wrong motivational methods. Therefore, I've set myself the big goal to change that with this book. I cannot repeat it often enough: in times that are becoming ever more uncertain, people—with their individual personalities—will be the most important success factor of the future. That also means that we need to radically change the prevailing approach to motivation. When we truly understand what motivates, moves, and drives people, we hold in our hands the key to a life of satisfaction, success, and purpose.

In each of us lies a dormant need to make changes, to experience bold breakthroughs, and to enjoy personal freedom.

"Oh come on, Ilja. That almost sounds like a revolution." Yes, you're right. I agree. That was my intention: to blow the wind of change through rigid businesses, stuffy offices, and lives that are determined by others. To initiate a revolution in motivation that will send the know-it-all blowhards packing and ensure that we are, once again, finally driven by meaningful motivations. Sounds ambitious? Correct, because I simply have no interest in mediocre goals anymore. At the end of the day, each of us has a great need to make changes, to experience bold breakthroughs, and to enjoy personal freedom. So out with the old and in with the new. Let's define an internal motivation beyond the carrot and the stick, characterized instead by purpose and values. It would make me immensely grateful if you would help me carry this philosophy out into the world and infect others with the positive change virus.

It all starts with a firm kick in the butt. And in your own. In order to be able to do this in the best possible way, we first want to devote ourselves to the simple—but equally crucial—question of what, exactly, motivation is. For, although this term is constantly on everyone's lips, there's a great semantic vagueness that prevails about it. So let's daringly attempt to define it.

AN UNCOMFORTABLE TRUTH

Okay, what exactly is behind the concept of motivation? Purely linguistically, it can be traced back to the Latin word, *movere* (to move, to drive). Wikipedia defines it as "The reason for people's actions, desires, and needs. Motivation is also one's direction to behavior, or what causes a person to want to repeat a behavior."[22] I don't know about you, but these sentences are a bit too complicated for me. So let me introduce my own, much simpler, definition:

Motivation is the inner drive to move from point A to point B, physically or mentally.

I would like to emphasize one fact in this sentence particularly clearly—namely, that motivation always comes from within. Even if the term "external motivation" is used in almost every article, book, or seminar, any drive brought about by the "carrot and stick" method is a type of "motivation" in theory only. In practice, external motivation—where people only act on the basis of money, praise, or avoidance of punishment—is no more than a myth. "But wait, Ilja. What about the Klinsmann example, salary increases, or bonus payments for reaching goals?" Of course, this objection is justified. After all, rewards in the form of money, property, or recognition—as well as the threat of punishments—definitely have a corresponding effect. Unfortunately, this effect is always short-lived. If you've ever unsuccessfully tried to use the prospect of an ice cream treat or the threat of an iPad ban to get your child to tidy up their room, then you'll know what I mean.

The same principle also applies to our professional life. No amount of money or bonus payment in the world will help you over the long term to do a job that frustrates you, makes you ill, or that you have no passion for. Similarly, in the long run, any threat of termination, sanctions, or loss of hierarchical status fizzles out. In the short term, you're motivated, full of energy and zest for action, but as soon as the effect wears off, you fall back to the original level—often, even, significantly lower. The result: the dosage and intensity of the external stimulus must be continuously increased. It's a little bit like a drug addict who is never satisfied and needs more and more stuff to reach his feel-good level. The reason is that the more frequently "carrot and stick" are used as a supposed external motivation, the faster the corresponding effect wears off. In this case, one can also talk about the point of diminishing marginal returns. You may ask, "What is that?" Imagine entering your local pub after a hot day. The first beer is heaven on earth for you, and you would pay anything for it. This probably goes the same for the second one. By the third, your enthusiasm is already subsiding. And after the eighth one, you no longer even want to look at a beer and would rather grab the water instead. That's exactly the principle of diminishing marginal returns.

Because this is the case, long-term, meaningful, and sustainable motivation always comes from within. A deep need, a value to be fulfilled, or a specific motivation will ensure that we act, and then will also lead to the corresponding external results. Let me pronounce a potentially painful truth:

You cannot motivate other people!

So, now it's out, and I can sense the oncoming storm of protests and indignation. Believe me, no other statement of mine triggers more controversial discussions in companies than this one. No wonder. After all, we have all learned over the years that with the right combination of carrot and stick we can drive our employees, colleagues, and business partners to unprecedented high performance. But, as with other things in life, in this case, there are always two people involved: the person who motivates and the one who wants to be motivated. And there's one word in that statement that's critical. Because if someone doesn't want to do something, under any circumstances, then your methods can be as modern, attractive, or sophisticated as can be: they won't stand a chance. I'd like to expand the above sentence a bit to make the statement even clearer:

You cannot motivate other people if they don't want to be motivated!

Of course, the same applies vice versa: other people cannot motivate us if we don't want that. Have I shaken your world view too much now? Do you completely disagree? I want to remind you that I'd like you to consider my ideas, opinions, and approaches as critically as possible. Check my statement against your everyday life. However, I predict that when you use external motivational skills, many people will be resistant to it. For, as much as I would like it to be otherwise:

People only change for reasons that are important to them, and never the ones that we would like them to.

Does this mean that every motivation is always a type of self-motivation? In principle, yes. We cannot motivate others if they don't want it. But if we understand that this is just how it goes, then at the end of the day, it's all the same. We'll look at exactly how that works in the course of the next chapter. In short, the solution is: if we want to motivate other people to move mentally or physically from point A to point B, then we need to know their inner motives and create the framework conditions in which they are triggered as often as possible—provoked or nudged, that is. At first glance, this sounds easier than it actually is, because it requires maximum flexibility as the motivator and the presence of the following three characteristics:

1. A real interest in the other party
2. The ability to be a good listener
3. The willingness to put one's own motivations aside in support of the desired results

The better you know the values, needs, and motivations of your employees, colleagues, and customers, the more flexibly you can align your communication and, thus, motivate them to change. But there is one important point to keep in mind.

SIX-PACKS, GOLF, AND FULL BANK ACCOUNTS

So motivation is the inner drive to move from point A to point B physically or mentally. Basically, this can happen in two ways: either because point A has become unbearable for us, or because alternative B sounds a lot more enticing. We always change when the pain has become too great, or when we are driven by an unbridled desire for growth, happiness, and joy. And that's why we either move away from a problem or toward an opportunity. That is the essence of every change.

I would like to explain this to you with a practical example. Think about the last time you bought a perfume. As you strolled along the luxury counters in your department store of choice, the shopping mall, or a local retailer, you sought advice from attractive women and tested for a long time until, at some point, you took a chance on—according to the sales figures—typically either Chanel No. 5, Dior Poison, or Yves Saint Laurent Mon Paris.

We always need the correct drive to be able to—or to want to—think, decide, and act differently.

However, there are a lot of problem buyers in this segment. This has fascinated me again and again every year at Christmas time in the perfume departments of my department stores. What do you think were the top sellers there year after year? I want to tell you. They were Old Spice, 4711 Eau de Cologne, and Irish Moss. Of course, everything in a pretty gift wrap with a bow around it. If you ask yourself, "How can so many people have such bad taste?" then here's the solution to that riddle. More than 75 percent of December sales were regularly made on Christmas Eve, between ten in the morning and two in the afternoon. Because the customers had waited so long, all of the good stuff was by then already sold out. They didn't take action until the problem had become overwhelming. The gentlemen among my readers will understand this: "What? Noon already? Then I guess I better mosey on out to get some presents!"

That is motivation in its classic form. Either we are attracted by opportunities, or problems push us. And even if the method of motivation always has a stronger power, in the long term, we always need goals, dreams, and visions to move toward. Whether we want to avoid pain or experience joy, without the right drive, you simply cannot think differently, decide differently, or act differently. In today's world, that is synonymous with stasis, stagnation, and regression. Only those who grow as a person, develop themselves, and constantly learn will succeed in the markets of tomorrow. The key to this is the proper motivation. However, this is never an end in itself, but always the necessary basis for desired changes. Without the right drive, there is no personal development, we do not grow, and we do not improve as a company. And even if we manage to advance toward our goals, it's unclear whether we can last until the end, because nothing else we do is as difficult for us as the sustained implementation of change. For instance, the last diet, the gym membership, and the repeated attempts to quit smoking. Short-term success is no problem at all. Guided by the initial euphoria, we effortlessly start on our way. However, you soon get caught up in the routine and make a few initial exceptions—and before you know it, the old habits have gained the upper hand again. But why is that?

In my lectures, I like to ask my audience a question at this point. "How many of you would like to get more exercise?" Almost always, all hands go up here. Then I probe further: "How many of you would like to lose a few pounds?" Again, I regularly observe an almost 100 percent positive response rate. But the next question is decisive: "How many of you know exactly what you need to do to achieve that?" At this point, a murmur usually spreads through the hall as the first several feel caught and look down. So you probably already suspect the question that comes next: "And how many of you do that every day?" If I look at the audience at this point, I see a maximum of two or three hands in the air. The rest, unfortunately, must admit that, although all the necessary information is available to them, the change is not consistently implemented. This is precisely the big dilemma. There's never too little knowledge. It's always because we don't consistently apply the existing knowledge. I'm sorry if I've burst your bubble, but it's true.

If information, knowledge, and understanding were the deciding factors in our motivation to change, then each of us would have a six-pack stomach, play golf all day23, and dive happily like Scrooge McDuck through our endless cash reserves every morning.

For more than fifteen years, I've been exploring the subject of personality development and studying with increasing fascination how people tick and what drives and motivates them. My main finding can be wonderfully summed up in one sentence:

Everyone wants change. But nobody wants to change.

Have you had similar experiences? Do you also know people who are dissatisfied with everything, who find nothing suitable, and who would like to change their company, society, and the whole world from one day to the next? You can't imagine how many of these types of contemporaries I know who know exactly what and who would have to change around them, just so they can stay the way they are.

One of the best examples of this attitude was one of my coworkers at Karstadt; let's call her Erika Grating. If I saw her in the morning in the corridor and asked her, "So, Mrs. Grating, how are you today?" the answer almost always came back in a whiny and frustrated tone: "Hah, another eight hours and then we'll finally have made it through again." Erika Grating had two standard phrases for which she was known. If there was a problem somewhere, she basically said, "Somebody needs to do something about that." And if you came back to her with something like, "Yes, but why don't you do anything?" then she used standard phrase number two: "Who, me? Please, Mr. Grzeskowitz, I can't take on any more work. The others should do it." We all know people like Erika Grating, right? When everyone is waiting for others to do something, nothing ever happens.

Fortunately, the opposite is true. A single person can make a huge difference when we are ready to take responsibility. For our thoughts. For our actions. For our life. This requires only a consistent decision. Either we can be a changemaker who actively shapes the increasingly intense transformation, or we can be a plaything of external circumstances. And yes, I am well aware that in my books I point out nothing else as often as the importance of taking responsibility. But it still doesn't seem to be enough. Just today, I saw a review of my book, *Think it. Do it. Change it. How to Dream Big, Act Bold and Get the Results You Want*, in which the reviewer wrote: "In general, the book was good. Unfortunately, the motivation stayed with me only about a week. You probably have to read it over again." At that moment, I thought of another great saying by the great Zig Ziglar, who once said, "People often say that motivation doesn't last. Well, neither does bathing—that's why we recommend it daily." Whether we like it or not, it's always we ourselves who are responsible for implementing our plans. Not our boss, not our family, and not the author of a book. (It should be noted that having the right people around you will, of course, have a decisive effect, but more on that later.) The all-important question is, therefore:

EVERY FOOL IS DIFFERENT

As a frequent flyer, I know the airports of the world like the back of my hand. Every single city has its peculiarities and its very special charm. One of my favorites is the Cologne Bonn Airport. If you've already experienced arriving there, then you know that on the way to the exit, you walk along a wall on which the entire text of the Basic Laws of the Rhineland is printed. Every single slogan is prominently displayed there, which immediately puts you in a positive mood and has you looking forward to the great people in Cologne. But, while I would not necessarily buy into some of these "laws" ("*It comes as it comes,*" "*So far it has always gone well,*" or "*If we do not know, we do not need to, so continue on with it!*"), there is one sentence that always fascinates me. No, I'm not talking about the famous "*Will you drink one with me?*" but about the headline of this section: "*Every fool is different.*"

Every person is different. Every person is individual. Every person is a unique personality with strengths, weaknesses, and of course, lovable quirks. "But Ilja," you may now object, "that's a common platitude." And you're right about that. Nevertheless, I'd like to emphasize the importance of this statement as clearly as possible and to look at it a little more closely with you. Even if just about every human being vehemently asserts that it's quite clear that every person is an individual, the actual behavior, unfortunately, looks completely different. Pretend you're a little mouse in your cafeteria, your favorite restaurant, or a subway car, and listen to the conversations of your fellow human beings (of course, very discreetly, since no one likes to be eavesdropped on). You'll quickly notice a prevalent behavioral pattern.

The standard formula for communication is: what applies to me must also apply to all others.

Using this subconscious pattern, personal opinions, views, and beliefs are imposed on the conversation and declared to be universally valid with complete disregard for the harm done to the conversational partner. The result: one doesn't listen to the other at all, they talk at each other and complain afterward about how bad our modern communication is.

Let's take a deeper look now at the "Every fool is different" philosophy. What makes each of us unique as a person? Why are we the way we are? And why is it that even identical twins can have two completely different characters, even though they are genetically almost identical? The answer is given in the following figure:

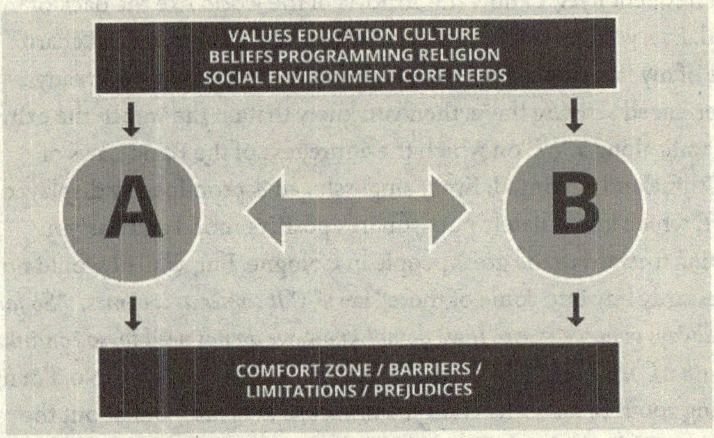

The Model of Individual Personalities

A and B in this model represent two different people. Their individual personalities would be characterized by a variety of influences. Of course, there's the parenting, the family, and other important caregivers like the class teacher, the soccer coach, and the guitar instructor. Additionally, there's also the social environment, religion, and especially the culture: it makes a huge difference whether a child grows up as a Christian in a millionaire household in New York's Upper East Side, or as an atheist in a low-income household in the Bronx, where the child's bedroom is shared with six siblings. These factors have a strong influence on what values, beliefs, and core needs determine our behavior. The strongest imprinting of our personality takes place in childhood and continues until the teenage years. But even as adults, we're still exposed to a variety of influences that have a corresponding effect on what we are, think, and do.

Whenever two people communicate with each other, two different worlds meet.

The sum of all these factors and experiences ultimately forms our individual personality. And because this sum is not the same for any of the nearly eight billion people on this earth, every single one of us also lives in our own world, represented in the figure by the two circles. The greater our experience and knowledge, the larger the circle. In other words, each of us has boundaries that are defined by our comfort zone, limitations, and prejudices. Now comes the decisive point. Whenever two people communicate with each other, two different worlds meet. With different values, different experiences, and very individual prejudices, limitations, and boundaries. Nevertheless, 99 percent of all conversations proceed according to the formula previously mentioned: "What applies to me, of course, must apply to everyone else." What a mistake. Just because something is true for A doesn't mean it has to be true for B. Just because a certain value is important for A doesn't mean that it is the same for B. And just because A can't imagine something, it could still be that B already has three possible solutions in mind.

I can already hear your objection. "Come on, Ilja, it's clear that every human being lives in his own individual world." Believe me, I understand, because I hear this phrase in many variations over and over again. But if it's so clear, then why do so many sales pitches fail? Why are more and more relationships going down the drain? And why do so many people have difficulty developing deep and sustainable motivation? Quite simply because this model is so incredibly simple in principle, but extremely complicated in its daily use. So even in this case, the Above Average Effect[24] operates, which says that the majority of people think they are smarter, stronger, better, etc., than the average, even if the objective criteria say otherwise. For example, have you ever noticed that 90 percent of motorists claim to be good at driving, but 90 percent of motorists seem to have won their driving license in a lottery? I leave the percentage calculation to you.

Those who want change first have to change themselves.

It's in the nature of man that we want to be right and we move forward with blinders on and proselytize to other people with our views. Additionally, many of us are just very bad listeners. So we turn around ourselves, with a mode of communication like a one-way street, and we become immune to ideas and views from the outside. As your own limitations, prejudices, and beliefs grow stronger, the boundaries of your individual world increasingly shift inward. A vicious circle that sooner or later leads to dogmatism, a know-it-all attitude, and at the same time, increasing dissatisfaction. The tragic thing is that dissatisfied people complain about everything and everyone, without realizing that the real problem is themselves—such as extremists on both the political left and right.

So I would like to repeat it again: *every fool is different*. Each person is unique. With individual values, experiences, and boundaries. You, as well as me, and every other person on this beautiful planet. Once you've not only understood this fact, but integrated it into your daily behavior, nothing will be the same as it once was.

You will communicate better, achieve better results, and at the same time, grow as a person, because you learn from others, think outside the box, and thereby push the boundaries of your own comfort zone further outward.

And that closes the circle. We've already determined that it's impossible to motivate other people, whereas it's extremely easy to demotivate them. Just as we need to be careful not to impose our model of the world on other people, we also have to stop trying to push others from the outside. Always remember, *Every fool is different,* and whoever doesn't want to change doesn't change. On the contrary, the more you attempt a crisp *Tschakka,* a tasty carrot, or a painful smack in these moments, the greater the resistance. A motivation based on a sense of purpose will work the exact opposite way. By starting with ourselves and inspiring others for our ideas. By meeting others according to their needs, values, and motives. Knowing these and combining them with personal goals creates a magical cocktail of deep drive, genuine commitment, and a contagious passion. Therefore, I would like to conclude this chapter with a kind of "rule of thumb" that wonderfully summarizes all the previous ideas:

Always go first.
Be the change.
If you are motivated, then you will motivate others.
If you are inspired, then you will inspire others.
If you change yourself, then everything changes around you.

All it takes is a brave look in the mirror and the irrefutable decision to take full responsibility for your life. Are you ready for that?

Changemaker's Memo: The Five Big Ideas from This Chapter

1. We are in the midst of a transformation from being an information-driven society to being a purpose-driven society.
2. Kick Your Own Ass: Kick yourself in the ass instead of waiting for others to motivate you.
3. Motivation is the inner drive to move from point A to point B physically or mentally.
4. You can't motivate other people if they don't want to be motivated.
5. Everyone wants change. But nobody wants to change themselves.

PART 3

The Persistence

CHAPTER 7

Change. Just. Do. It.

General Woo very nearly smiled.
Saw the light in the little child.
The prince and old lady shade.

—Peter Murphy, "The Prince and Old Lady Shade"

The biggest enemy of change is passivity. You can't imagine how many people I've worked with as a coach who have not put their goals, dreams, and hopes into action. And that's not because they are stupid, unmotivated, or even disadvantaged in any way. On the contrary. As a rule, they truly want to be successful, have the necessary knowledge, and work with me to develop a detailed, step-by-step implementation plan. But when I ask about the first results a few weeks later, they look at me with sad eyes and have not yet started on the plan. Instead, I hear the same excuses, why it wasn't possible, why the timing was wrong, and why they'd rather just wait and see. But this is the fatal mistake. Deep inside, these people unconsciously still hope that the desired changes will just happen, without them having to do anything for themselves. With an almost childlike naivety, they start from the mistaken belief that the external circumstances will change—as if by magic—because a knight on a white horse will come riding along out of nowhere.

The biggest brake on personality development is the tendency toward passivity.

Again and again in my seminars, I realize that the biggest brake on personality development is the tendency to wait, hesitate, and plan. I often feel that, in addition to all the content, the great atmosphere, and the many stimuli, my participants come to me for one reason only: to give them permission to begin the desired changes and to reassure them.

"Start finally. You have everything you need. You just have to get on with the doing."

On the one hand, I'm doing this with great joy because, for me, there's nothing more fulfilling than encouraging people to finally do what they want deep inside. On the other hand, I always feel a certain sadness in these moments, because nobody really needs the permission of other people to live out their dreams. Is it like this for you sometimes? In the end, it doesn't matter where the key trigger comes from, it's just important that you get started. No matter which area of your life you want different results in—whether on the job, financially, in your relationships, or health-wise—if you don't act and do the things you need to do differently, everything will remain the same. Are you dissatisfied with something? Please step away from the idea that the external circumstances and the people around you will change on their own. They don't. Your luck, your success, and your general satisfaction are top priorities. It's all up to you. And it's all within you. The sooner you internalize this fact, the better. That's why the following phrase is so incredibly important for you—make it your new daily mantra.

Change happens only when you change. If you don't, nobody will.

Do you remember what was said earlier? You are not the victim of the universe, you are the universe. You have all the resources you need to design it to your liking. My old employer, IKEA, would probably put it this way: are you already doing it, or are you still procrastinating?

Nothing would make me happier than for you to make the decision, here and now, to fight passivity and live your dreams. You may have all the knowledge in the world, and yet you are the one who has to act. You may have all the expertise in the world, but you yourself must make the change. Or, as Mahatma Gandhi put it, "Be the change you wish to see in the world." He was right, this great thinker and changemaker. Therefore,

I would like to begin this chapter with the three most important and, as it were, universal qualities of those who are doers. I'm talking about a powerful motivation, the willingness to focus on action, and a strong changemaker mentality that ensures lasting results. Or to put it more concisely:

The triad of implementation skills: Purpose—Taking Action—Mentality.

These three factors form the foundation for lasting success in every imaginable area of life. The first may seem self-explanatory, but without the absolute will to take your fate into your own hands, you will never be able to actively press ahead with change. It's therefore important to ask the following questions in order to gain the necessary clarity for your very personal purpose:

What do I want to achieve?
What is important to me?
What do I stand for?
What really drives me?

The answers then produce the corresponding goals, which are then to be focused on with maximum energy and passion. Only if you focus your energies without getting bogged down can you develop the important momentum that provides the necessary motivation to act in the next step. Of course, your general mentality also plays a crucial role. Because nothing is given for free in life, and whoever wants to achieve great things must be prepared to pay the appropriate price.

With these three qualities, you lay the foundation for a strong skill in implementation, for which you will be the envy of those around you. These qualities then have to be further developed step by step. So, in this chapter, I'll introduce you to a great tool that will help you get going faster. Then, we will look together at how to escape the perfection trap. And finally, we will dedicate ourselves to a factor that has often been overlooked—namely, the happiness we all so long for. It plays a big role when we're talking about success. But the good news is that we can accomplish this ourselves. Does that sound good? Then I'd like to wish you good luck! May it be your faithful companion.

IMPERFECT, BUT SEXY

Be completely honest here: are you sometimes inclined to fall into the perfection trap? I know only too well this biggest hindrance to success. And from my daily work, I know that the same goes for many people out there. What do I mean by this? I'm talking about the claim you make to yourself that you always have to be perfectly prepared. The mistaken belief that something could be missing. The fatal miscalculation of not being good enough. If you are still not sure whether you're affected by the symptoms of the perfection trap, there's an easy way to check it. In practice, the urge for perfectionism is primarily noticeable as follows. Instead of making a real decision,[25] setting a powerful goal, and then implementing it with motivation and passion, you prefer to put all of your available energy into preparation. You pile up knowledge, do research on the internet, and become a world champion in planning. Yep, and while others have long been underway already with their actions, you prefer to keep on planning. You prepare yourself for Day X, when you will finally want to get started. Of course, this is announced prominently, so that everyone knows what you are planning. Then you buy a huge stack of books (which, of course, you never read), take online courses, attend seminars, all the while talking over and over again about how you're not far away from it now, and after the holidays (alternatively: next month, after vacation, after the Christmas rush, the New Year, next season, or in autumn), you assume you will finally and definitely begin. Naturally, you don't do that, and instead continue planning further. You wait so long for the "perfect moment" that you miss taking the first crucial step toward implementation.

So now I want to tell you the big secret of success, change, and even life. The all-important puzzle piece for transforming from being the Planning World Champion to being the Conversion King. Are you ready? Really? Because once I say it, there's no going back. Okay, here we go.

The perfect moment will never come.

Something like the perfect time to start does not exist. The sooner you internalize this principle, the better. The perfect moment will never come. You will never feel fully prepared. There will always be something that you do not—and cannot—know, as well as something that you haven't considered. So what? Life is like that. Success is never a straight line that connects your actual present state to the goal, but an emotional process with many ups and downs. A road with obstacles to overcome, with many setbacks, unexpected challenges, and detours you never even dreamed of. And your job is to face this process and learn to evolve and grow as a person.

Allow yourself to make mistakes.

The trick here is to allow yourself to not be perfect and to make mistakes in order to learn from them. For a long time, I wondered how best to make this necessary mental switch possible. And I never thought that I would find the solution in politics—more specifically, through Berlin's famous "party mayor," Klaus Wowereit. Do you remember him? He had two really ingenious moments in his career (and we'll just sweep those many not-so-ingenious moments under the rug for now). First, he took the wind out of the sails of his political opponents right at the beginning of his term with his legendary "I'm gay—and that's a good thing!" speech. However, the much more relevant moment for our topic occurred in November 2003. During an interview with *FOCUS*, Wowereit was asked if money makes one sexy. His answer was to change the image of the German capital in a single moment, because when asked if there was a connection between wealth and erotic charisma, he replied, "No. You can see that in Berlin. We are poor, but sexy." This phrase later developed into Wowereit's famous slogan[26] and contributed significantly to the fact that, in the following years, the capital increasingly received the reputation of the "New York of the twenty-first century." Anyone who wanted to be a part of it moved to the Mitte, Prenzlauer Berg, or Friedrichshain neighborhoods.

The perfect moment will never come, so start today with the development of your character.

And now comes the exciting part, because the economic conditions of that time were really not perfect, and the citizens had to accept many cutbacks. However, the slogan "Poor, but sexy!" ensured that the people of Berlin were suddenly proud of their Kurfurstendamm, Hackescher Markt, and Friedrichstrasse neighborhoods. Sure, after all, everyone wants to be sexy, right? And this mental shift had corresponding consequences. The infamous Winds of Change blew through Berlin, and all over the world, the formerly dusty capital was suddenly considered innovative, cosmopolitan, and dynamic. Other metropolises certainly had better infrastructure, more sophisticated development concepts, and a greater financial strength, but Berlin had established a culture of change that London, Paris, and Madrid simply could not hold a candle to.

"Okay, Ilja. It might be nice that Berlin awakened from its Sleeping Beauty slumber, but I live in a little town that no one has heard of. What does that have to do with the perfection trap?" That's pretty easy to explain. In the year that Klaus Wowereit gave that famous interview to *FOCUS*, I had just moved from Hamburg to Berlin. So I was fortunate in that I was able to experience firsthand the transformation of this pulsating metropolis. And one thing has continued to fascinate me: although the times could be bad, the conditions still tough, and the prospects still gloomy, the people were always united. Full of pride, they proclaimed their new motto for life: "So what? We are poor, but sexy!" The more I was allowed to experience this mentality, the more I was fascinated by the resulting culture of change that spread through all social classes. And that is exactly the solution to our problem: to develop an attitude that allows one to make mistakes and be imperfect. One thing should be made clear over and over again. No matter how good a plan may be, once the first steps have been taken, there are unexpected obstacles, challenges, and setbacks that force us to readjust and improvise. Therefore, let's learn from Berlin and shout out into the world:

We may be imperfect, but we're damn sexy!

That's because we act, make courageous decisions, and go in directions that no one has gone before. Because our motto is:

Better to be imperfectly started than perfectly procrastinated.

Whatever goals you have set for yourself, free yourself from the perfection trap. Because you are good enough and have everything you need to start on the way to successful implementation. At some point, the moment comes when you finally have to start. It's better to be imperfectly started than perfectly procrastinated. Along the way, you will naturally make many mistakes, and you'll have to solve unforeseen problems and overcome obstacles. But first, that's how it is in life, and second, it's the only way to learn, grow, and develop. Here is my rule of thumb:

Prepare yourself as much as necessary, but as little as possible.

Then you start. Be satisfied with 80 percent, because you'll never achieve 100 percent anyway. Get going and learn along the way. The more you dare to start imperfectly, the more successful you will be. Or, as the Korean artist Nam June Paik put it so aptly, "When too perfect, God won't be happy!" I'll go one step further and add: we doers may be imperfect, but we're damn sexy. That's something that the hesitant, the cautious, and the perfection fetishist will never achieve, because while the others are all talking, we just do it. Isn't that right?

THE SEVEN-SECOND RULE

Did you know that the increasing digitization of our lifestyle has caused our attention spans to be lower than that of a goldfish? (Do I now have your full attention?) According to a Microsoft study from 2015,[27] this has decreased in the last few years from thirteen seconds (2013) down to just eight seconds, while the fish are still at nine. And while the original source used in the study is controversial, common sense tells us that it's getting harder and harder to process the many stimuli around us and to focus 100 percent on one thing. This also has a huge impact on your implementation skills. Although the neurosciences are far from the point of knowing everything about the human brain today, modern research is bringing more and more fascinating details to the surface. (And the usual statements like "the brain has two halves, one for logic and the other for creativity" or "we use only 10 percent of our brain capacity" are, unfortunately, not scientifically tenable but are still happily repeated mantras in motivational training mills. Which doesn't make them any more correct.)

In a fascinating experiment at the Max Planck Institute for Human Cognitive and Brain Sciences, Professor John-Dylan Haynes explored the processes that precede a rational decision in the brain.[28] In an interview after the experiment, he reported, "Many processes in the brain occur automatically and without involvement of our consciousness. This prevents our mind from being overloaded by simple routine tasks. But when it comes to decisions, we tend to assume they are made by our conscious mind. This is questioned by our current findings." (By the way, this is a wonderful example of critical thinking, which we will talk about later.) In the study, the participants were given a simple task. They were free to decide if they wanted to press a button in front of them with their right or left hand. They were instructed to make this decision without a time limit, but that they should keep in mind exactly when they did it, while the brain activities and processes were simultaneously measured. What was the result? Based on the measurements, the scientists were able to predict exactly how this would turn out seven seconds before the conscious decision was made. At this point, I'd like to quote Mr. Spock by saying, "Fascinating!" Let's allow this finding to sink in:

Our daily decisions have already been made on an unconscious level before we really register them with our full awareness.

Imagine if we were both getting to know each other in person for the first time. Now please count out loud, "7, 6, 5, 4, 3, 2, 1." Within this seven-second period, you've not only made a visual impression of me, but also matched it up against your internal assessment standards, preferences, and experiences, and you have formed an opinion. As a result, you either can sympathize with me, or on a subconscious level you cannot stand me. At the same time, you decide whether I can work competently, am humorous, or am eligible as a potential business or sexual partner. Now the circle closes, because the same unconscious process determines whether you procrastinate or act in a particular situation. Whenever you feel an impulse to say, do, or make anything, without your consciously controlling it, your brain works at full speed for seven seconds. It answers questions like, "What negative experiences have I faced in the past?", "What could go wrong?", "What do my colleagues think?", or

"Am I good enough?" You know what I'm talking about, don't you? If not, just think back to the moment when, as a younger person, you were out at a club and chose your supposed dream partner. Even though the butterflies in your stomach cried out to you, "Let's go, talk!" nothing actually happened. That's because the Seven-Second Rule thwarted you.

The Seven-Second Rule is the perfect implementation program for your projects.

If you have not acted within the seven seconds, then nothing will happen. On the contrary, your brain will talk you out of it. You'll procrastinate, find excuses, or become distracted by other activities. And the more you respond in this way, the more normal it becomes—until, at some point, a strong habit will even have developed out of it. Please keep in mind that all of this happens unconsciously and automatically. The majority of people don't even know that they have downloaded and installed for themselves a wonderfully reliable program for procrastination and passivity.

Fortunately, you can also use this finding to train a wonderfully well-functioning implementation program. I call this tool the Seven-Second Rule. From now on, you should use this rule as often as possible. Beginning today, whenever you are triggered—to hold an important conversation with an employee, to call a difficult customer, to praise someone, to meet up with another person, or to put an idea into action—you have exactly seven seconds to work in any way to physically start the action.

Whenever you feel an impulse to do, say, or implement something, you have seven seconds to physically take action.

This doesn't necessarily have to be a big thing; it's also about helping you with the little things. Pick up the phone, write something down, make eye contact, or open your laptop to write the important email. The main thing is that you get moving. This is so important because the body and the mind are equal parts of the same system. If one half changes, then it has an effect on the other, and vice versa. I can't tell you how much the Seven-Second Rule has increased my implementation skills. The same goes for thousands of listeners in my audiences. And it can do the same for you. Initially, you should start the process as consciously as possible. You feel an impulse? Count backward to yourself, 7, 6, 5, 4, 3, 2, 1. And before you reach 1, you just do it. Whenever you are in a situation where you ask yourself, "Should I or shouldn't I?" count 7, 6, 5, 4, 3, 2, 1 to yourself. And then just do it.

Whenever a thought like "I'd prefer to do it later/tomorrow/next week/etc." is in your head, count 7, 6, 5, 4, 3, 2, 1. And then just do it. Over and over again. The more often you train this way, the sooner you will develop a powerful habit. Because every time you apply the Seven-Second Rule, you reprogram your unconscious automation from "procrastination" to "action." And before you know it, everyone around you will be referring to you as "that lucky devil." You just went through the transformation from Procrastinator to Doer. In fact, there is a direct correlation between the Seven-Second Rule and the frequency of the Luck Factor in your life. Why this works and how to make the best possible use of this relationship is explained in the next section. Are you ready? You now have seven seconds to start reading further. 7, 6, 5, 4, 3, 2, 1.

MAKE YOUR OWN LUCK

When I was a child, I was a huge fan of the funny mini comic books from Disney. What I loved was spending hours flipping through them under my bedcovers, excited to follow the adventures of Mickey Mouse, Goofy, or Chief O'Hara. I was especially excited by the Duck family. There was Scrooge McDuck, who with only one dime of startup capital became the richest man in Duckberg and spent his days strolling through his numerous money chambers. The three groomed nephews—Huey, Dewey, and Louie—scrambled around the Junior Woodchucks scouting camp, while the beautiful Daisy played mind games with her two admirers—Donald Duck and Gladstone Gander. Those two latter characters could not be more different. On the one hand, there was the likeable (though completely clumsy) Donald, who seemed to be stuck with bad luck nipping at his heels, while his arrogant and lazy cousin Gladstone seemed to be persecuted by one lucky streak after another. I still remember, as if it were yesterday, that I wished for nothing more than to someday be able to lead a similar lifestyle as the lucky duck with the quiff hairstyle.[29] In my mind's eye, I already saw myself lying in the hammock on my porch, while earning my living with lottery winnings, finding diamonds, or receiving letters with cash.

Today, scarcely thirty-five years later, I still think the Duck family is really great, and as my children now also read the funny paperbacks, I even have the opportunity to peruse them once in a while. However, I have learned and internalized an important lesson in life:

Everything that is worth achieving is the result of diligence, hard work, and persistence.

Nothing—absolutely nothing—truly falls from the sky into our lap. Everything that is consumed must be produced beforehand. Everything you spend must be earned beforehand. And everything you want to take has to be given by someone else—if you happen to be a politician, I'd like you to read this paragraph very carefully. What still interests me as an adult is the topic of luck, for isn't the world full of Donalds and Gladstones? Don't you, too, know people whose bad luck seems to stick to their boots while others pull one lucky streak after another into their lives? At this point, we should address an important question: does the Luck Factor play a role when it comes to success in the most diverse areas of life? The ostensible answer to this is a clear *No*. When you look at successful people, you can always see the same ingredients that have led to their extraordinary results: brave ideas, diligence, hard work, willingness to make mistakes, persistence, and the ability to make other people aware of their own vision in order to inspire them. Even science cannot find a correlation between success and luck, and so Wikipedia defines luck as "the experience of notably positive, negative, or improbable events."[30] It also notes that "Carl Jung coined the term synchronicity, which he described as a 'meaningful coincidence.' " And coincidence is defined as being "a remarkable concurrence of events or circumstances that have no apparent causal connection with one another."[31] From an objective point of view, it seems that luck plays only a minor role in personal development, and alleged experts like to use this finding to proclaim that success can be planned.

But common sense tells us that something must be wrong. Life can't be designed on a drawing board, and of course, there are quite a few people who owe their success to lucky coincidences. In the old Scrooge McDuck manner, they were just in the right place at the right time, meeting the right people and having an idea whose moment had come. At the same time, there are a number of factors that dramatically increase the chances that you will have luck.

The Luck Factor plays an important role in having success. The good news is that we can influence this factor ourselves.

"Sure, Ilja, then how? I thought that luck was a random factor, so how can I influence it?" Before I introduce you to four very concrete methods, I'd like to present you with another less mathematical but more practical definition:

Luck results when hard work meets the right opportunity.

Increase the likelihood that you will be favored by luck.

It is indeed possible to create one's own luck. The more active we are—trying things out, making mistakes, and expanding our network—the higher the likelihood that someday the opportunity will come that we can later call luck. But the opposite is actually the case, because it is only—*de facto*—the reward for your tireless efforts. For this reason, the luck of the bold and the brave—as well as the renowned last-minute "Bayern-luck" of Munich's soccer team—is, in reality, hard work. Because if you create twice as many chances per game as your opponent, then the probability that a ball will luckily hit the goal is twice as high. Woody Allen put it in a nutshell when he said, "80 percent of success in life is just showing up." And that's exactly how it is. If you sit at home on the couch waiting to finally be lucky, life will be bitterly disappointing. However, those who open up, actively change, and work hard for their dreams will inevitably experience moments that look like luck from the outside. Unfortunately, you can never plan when that will be. However, I would now like to introduce four factors that significantly increase the likelihood of it happening sooner rather than later. I call them the Luck Boosters, and here they are:

Luck Booster #1: The Freedom of Commitment

I realize that it sounds weird, but in fact, the greatest possible freedom is to commit yourself. If you look around, however, you can discover the opposite pattern. No one wants to make decisions anymore, because they want to keep their options open. This applies to relationships, as well as projects or your daily job. The motto: initially, I invest only 80 percent, because who knows whether or not something better will come along. But the opposite is the case. The more you decide to do something from the top of your head to the tips of your toes, the more you will experience an unimagined inner freedom, because in this way, you commit yourself and focus all your energy on it. I have a very simple system that helps me to clearly define my priorities. Whenever I face a difficult decision, I choose between two options: either I say *Oh yeah!* from my heart to a choice (and, of course, to all the consequences that result from it, the positive as well as the negative), or I decide to say *no*. There is nothing in between for me, because I said goodbye to all the wishy-washy decisions a long time ago. My internal freedom meter thanks me every day. Because only those who commit themselves are truly free.

Say "Oh yeah!" or "No." There's nothing in between.

Luck Booster #2: Feeling Good without a Reason

As I write these lines, I find myself on a cruise ship moored in Lisbon, and one thing comes to my notice every day. Even though the sea is just beautiful, the food is delicious, and the weather is gorgeous, most of the people around me are in three different modes: talking about past journeys, planning for next year's, or complaining about the conditions on the current trip. The latter are the kind of people you know who, even in the most beautiful sky, discover a small cloud that will then ruin their day. It goes without saying that these nagging companions completely fail to enjoy the present. I probably notice it so much because I'm traveling with the two biggest role models I know: my two daughters, Emma and Elisabeth. You can't imagine with what curiosity, joy, and gratitude the two have enjoyed each and every moment of the journey. One day, when Elisabeth once again came to our cabin beaming with happiness, I asked her, "What's wrong with you? Why are you glowing like that?" Her answer was both naive and exemplary, "For no special reason, Papa!" This brings me to an important question:

When was the last time you felt good without a reason?

Just because you can. What, you can't remember? Then you should change that as quickly as possible, because your overall quality of life crucially depends on your ability to feel good for no reason.

Decisions we make from a negative frame of mind never lead to positive results.

Really, never. Or have you ever made a good decision from a bad frame of mind? If, on the other hand, we make decisions based on joy, abundance, and gratitude, then the results will match. So learn to feel good. As often as possible. By not living in the past or the future, but always enjoying the moment.[32] The more you are able to do this for the most part—and for no reason at all—the more you will be able to enjoy the situations in which an external factor makes your life more beautiful, intense, and happy.

Luck Booster #3: Identify the Wolf in Sheep's Clothing

Remember the fairy tale of Little Red Riding Hood? There we have a little girl with a basket of food on her way to her grandmother. She actually has a clear goal and knows exactly which way she must go. But then the bad wolf suddenly appears in different disguises along the way and distracts her. We know how it ends, because a short time later, Little Red Riding Hood is eaten by the wolf, who is disguised as the grandmother. And if you're wondering why I'm telling you about a fairy tale right now, then let me clarify: even in your everyday life, the evil wolf is always lurking on the sidelines. What, have you never noticed? No wonder; he has no gray fur and sharp teeth but appears in a variety of disguises instead.

I'm talking about the many time-killers, distractions, and supposed shortcuts that so often dissuade you from your real purpose. Because, honestly, how often are you occupied only with unimportant things, instead of devoting yourself to productively focusing on your important goal? How often do you work on a project, but your thoughts are somewhere else? How many times have you wanted to tackle an important task, but you went and checked your Facebook feed again? How often could you not give your children the necessary attention during a trip together, because you were also answering work-related emails? In all of these cases, the evil wolf tries to lure you off the beaten track so he can finally eat you. To increase your personal luck, you should learn to identify the wolf in your everyday life and not be distracted. Eliminate your time-killers, focus, and do only one task at a time. Remember the sentence that I introduced to you for the first time several pages ago:

"If you're in the room, be in the room!"

When you are in the room, be in the room. I don't know any philosophy that would be better suited to identifying the most diverse wolves in your everyday life and committing yourself 100 percent to a cause. Concentrate on what really matters. With your skin and your hair. And just let go of the rest. Your results will thank you.

Luck Booster #4: Be Positive. Always!

I don't believe in anything as much as in the power of a positive attitude. Do you even know a single negative person who has ever made a positive difference? You see...

Under the same conditions, it's always the inner attitude that makes the difference between success or failure, good or great, and luck or misfortune.

Naturally, this doesn't mean that you—like one of these light-and-love gurus—walk through life wearing rose-colored glasses, simply ignoring problems, and whitewashing the challenges of everyday life. On the contrary, problems are a part of life. What matters is how we handle them. The rule of thumb is to recognize the problem and, at the same time, think about how best to solve it. In this way, you always think in possibilities and never in limitations. You act from a mentality of abundance and kick to the curb those thoughts based on lack. Above all, *you* change, instead of hoping that the external circumstances change. Please never forget one thing: your attitude is not insignificant. It is everything, because it determines your basic approach, your ability to recognize opportunities, and—above all—your satisfaction in life. I hope that you'll never forget the three golden rules of a successful attitude:

Rule 1: Always be positive.
Rule 2: Always be positive.
Rule 3: Always be positive.

The world is full of negative, frustrated, and miserable people. But it's always the positive changemakers that lift it daily and make a decent mark on the universe.

With these four boosters, you'll be able to quickly raise your personal Luck Factor. But of course, luck is not just something you have or that comes to you. It is, above all, a state of being. Possibly, even, the one we humans strive for most. But the overwhelming majority of people make the crucial mistake of considering luck as something determined by external factors. What a mistake. Luck is never a goal that one can reach when certain things happen, when one possesses material things, or one experiences something. Luck is something completely different. It's a basic attitude toward life. A conscious choice. A "lucky attitude." Try it out today and be lucky. Without any reason. Simply because you can.

Changemaker's Memo:
The Five Big Ideas from This Chapter

1. Change happens only when you change. If you don't do it, nobody will.
2. The perfect moment will never come. Therefore, it's better to be imperfectly started than perfectly procrastinated.
3. Use the Seven-Second Rule to train your changemaker mentality.
4. Luck results when hard work meets the right opportunity.
5. There are four boosters that you can use to create your own luck; apply these to yourself. Learn to feel good for no reason. Identify the wolf in sheep's clothing. And be positive. Always!

CHAPTER 8

Success Is an Asshole

I wake up in the morning, and the sun begins to shine.
The day did sneak up on the night.
I see your face and I see myself, and I get a little taste of life.
I try to stand it for a while.
But I'm in a trance.

—The Scorpions, "In Trance"

"Success is an asshole!" I spat this sentence with contempt into the reflection of my face in the mirror. It was a New Year's Eve, many years ago. At that time, I was still managing director at Karstadt, and I was fresh in a new city after another transfer. Despite it being a special day, as usual, I had worked long hours and didn't return to my apartment until around seven. I felt a certain trepidation. No wonder, because it was the first time I would spend the turn of the new year completely alone. In a city that I didn't choose, and in which I didn't know a single person. While all over the city, parties sprang up, corks popped, and boisterous laughter seeped into my ears, my evening schedule looked the complete opposite. First, a pizza from a delivery service, a six-pack of beer to wash it down, then a little TV watching, and a toast with myself at midnight. An absolute low point in my life, because I had never felt so lonely and empty. And this was at a time when everyone around me would have described me as being very successful. This was no surprise, since from the outside I was actually something of a high flier, who had taken the career ladder by storm and achieved everything that others could only dream of. There was only one giant problem: if that was true, then why was I so frustrated on the inside?

If you don't achieve what you'd hoped to, there's only one person responsible, and that is you, yourself.

Suddenly, my negative emotions overcame me, and I became convinced that success is an asshole. Because if this was the price you had to pay for success in life, then I definitely did not want to be successful. I went to bed depressed and then stumbled back onto the hamster wheel two days later. Today, I am very grateful for that New Year's Eve, because my absolute low point was also a turning point in my life. It was as if a switch had been dropped into my lap. I understood for the first time that my frustration had nothing to do with external circumstances but was solely the result of my own choices that I had made over the previous few years—and, of course, the choices I had not made. Success wasn't the asshole, but only I, myself. Because I had let myself be guided by a definition of success that wasn't mine. Because I had not owned my own story for a long time, and I had oriented myself toward the expectations of others. There was only one person who could change that: me. So I promised myself that I would change myself. Not just a little, but radically. No more accepting compromises, but finally doing my own thing. This was not an overnight success, because I first had to find out what I really wanted. But the seeds were sown, and even today I am still harvesting, because I have learned three things:

1. It's never the shiny, blinking, and glamorous moments in our lives that shape our character. It's the low points, because these are almost always turning points.
2. Dissatisfaction, defeat, or frustration can be extremely powerful sources of motivation if we succeed in transforming those powerful emotions into productivity and a corresponding "Now more than ever" mentality.
3. Success is an individual thing that each person defines differently.

Yes, now it's time to get down to business, because I want to talk to you in this chapter about the word that I wrongly called an asshole so many years ago. No other topic has been written about in so many books, lectures, and published articles. Entrepreneur Darren Hardy has even paid it a printed tribute with one of the most successful magazines in the world.[33] And I'd like to now start off with a very personal question: would you describe yourself as successful? Not so easy to answer, is it? In fact, success is much more complex than what we are always sold as a prototype in the media. I mean the fat bank account, the Rolex on the wrist, the stellar career, the Porsche in the garage, the yacht in the port of Monaco, and an overall life marked by luxury and status symbols. Look at any ad of your choice, or walk through any shopping mall, and you'll understand what I'm talking about.

Avoid living a life that is in conflict with your identity.

But it is precisely this definition of success—based on external factors and recognition from others—that leads more and more people to chase after goals that aren't their own. They follow the dictates of fashion, succumbing to the temptations promulgated by modern media, and subtly but steadily move away from their own values, beliefs, and dreams. And that makes for extreme dissatisfaction in the long run, because you subconsciously feel that you are leading a life that is in conflict with your own identity.

After all, can success really only be tied to material things, external achievements, and the attainment of socially-decreed goals? Is it not also success if a single mother raises her three children while, at the same time, working two jobs and still being happy and satisfied? Is it not also success if a family decides to live far away from the big city in an old farmhouse and be completely self-sufficient? And is it not also success for a flourishing lawyer to give up his career, live on ten dollars a day as a diving instructor in Thailand, but to have finally found peace of mind through this activity? These are just three examples out of millions of others who clearly demonstrate one thing: success always comes from the inside out. For example, when we have put a project into action, achieved a goal that was important to us, or made a significant decision. Above all, success is always linked to our entire personal Change Diamond. Ultimately, it's your identity, your values, and your beliefs that determine what really matters to you in life. Of course, money and material things always play a certain role; all those people who want to convince you that money isn't important are not telling you the truth. But it must not be alienated as an end in itself. Because the factors responsible for happiness, satisfaction, and fulfillment are usually found on a completely different level.

So I'd like to ask you the same question that I also put to my coaching clients:

What does success mean for you?

At this point in the book, you should already have some clarity about what really matters to you, what drives you, and what makes your life meaningful. This will be very useful to you in answering the question, and I cannot stress enough how important this intense reflection is for your personal future. Do I have to point out once again that you absolutely must be radically honest with yourself? As always, here, too, you can fool the people around you for a while. But the person who looks back at you every morning in the mirror senses very clearly when the external appearance and the inner being are profoundly out of harmony.

Now, to put our money where our mouth is, let's have some facts: What is your very personal definition of success? Is it a skyrocketing career in a global corporation? The dream of having your own company? Or maybe a harmonious family life in the countryside with five children, a large collection of pets, and a private yard?

Please ignore all thoughts of other people, extrinsic expectations, or social conformity. It is your life and your satisfaction, and thus, your definition of success. "Okay, Ilja, but I find fast cars, a lot of cash, and an international jet-setter life to be pretty sexy." Wonderful. If money and material things are important to you, then you do everything you can to get as much as possible. But if it's something completely different, then please give these needs the appropriate space. I myself enjoy the luxurious aspects of life again and again. I collect nice (and, unfortunately, expensive) watches, I prefer to stay in the Ritz-Carlton when traveling instead of generic motels in the commercial area, and I spend money on nothing as much as I do for good food in excellent restaurants. Each time, it fills me with gratitude that I have worked to be able to afford these luxuries. But I don't need these amenities to be happy, and I could live without them at any time. This awareness alone dramatically increases my personal degree of freedom.

The better you know what's important to you, the better you can also fill the empty word "success" with the appropriate content. And this puts you in the position to align your life, your job, and your daily activities in order to be successful in all these areas. In order to give you the best possible support, I'd like to offer you my success formula, which you can use for every conceivable definition of success. I would like to conclude my introduction to this chapter with a mantra that has served me faithfully quite often, and that can do the same for you. It is:

If it feels good, it can't be that bad!

There's a lot to it, right?

THE SUCCESS FORMULA

The particular and individual definition of success is the indispensable foundation for happiness and satisfaction in life. In order to be able to be permanently—and especially simply—successful, we now want to fill the abstract concept of success with life and transform it into concrete results with the appropriate deeds. The bottom line is that success results from the consistent and constant repetition of supposedly small things. And that is why this is my totally personal success formula[34]:

Success = Clarity X Focus X Hard Work

Genuine and sustainable success is always the result of these three factors. It starts with a deep clarity about what is important to you. Next is unwavering focus on the necessary factors. And if you then combine these two qualities with hard, motivated, and—in particular—long-term work, then success will almost inevitably set in. Therefore, let's take a closer look at the individual components of the success formula.

Success Factor Number 1: Clarity

As children, we often played Cowboys and Indians. Each of us had his preferences about which role we wanted to play in our afternoon activities. However, at that time, we didn't have much choice, simply because we did not have the appropriate role models. So some played the Apache Chief Winnetou, while others preferred to be Marshal Matt Dillon—the protagonist from the cool TV series *Gunsmoke*. Nowadays, there are as many superheroes as there are grains of sand in the ocean (my favorites are clearly Batman, Ironman, and Rocket Raccoon of *Guardians of the Galaxy*), and when I watch my kids play, it's not so much a question of which role they want to play, but an entirely different question: *"Which superpower would you like to have?"*

Figure out what you want and what's important to you and makes you happy. Then you'll make the right decisions.

In the answers that follow the question, you can see their eyes start to radiate. Mind-reading, invisibility, time travel, speed, flying, or the ability to move objects with the power of the mind are just a few of the things children want these days. What would your answer be if I asked you this question? Which would be your preferred superpower? My choice would probably surprise you, because I would choose clarity. No other trait is of such crucial importance when it comes to living a fulfilled and contented life. Clarity is also essential to our individual definition of success. Only if you know what you want, what is important to you, and what makes you truly happy—and, of course, what you don't want, what isn't important to you, and what makes you unhappy—can you make the decisions that are necessary for you to get it.

If you've used the previous chapters to take a bold look in the mirror, then you should already have a high degree of clarity at this point. If, on the other hand, you are still a bit uncertain, then I recommend that you once again, intensively, read through the second chapter, "What's Important." The bottom line is that your own degree of clarity stands and falls by answering the questions of what really counts in life and what, exactly, you expect from it. And then there's a special domino effect that always fascinates me. I was able to marvel at it when it happened with myself, but also as it has worked with my customers. Clarity leads to more commitment in the first step, because the increased awareness of one's own values and what one really wants, of course, also makes itself felt in one's own communication. You make decisions more quickly, more transparently, and you provide guidance to the people around you. This increases your charisma and, ultimately, the efficiency you achieve in the different areas of your life.

Clarity => Commitment => Impact

But clarity offers yet another also very decisive side effect. Some folks like to call it having *Skin in the Game*, which is another way of saying *commitment*. If something is really important to you, then you do everything to make it happen. You invest time, energy, and money. You go the extra mile and stick with it even if you encounter hindrances or if your initial motivation wears off a bit. No matter what you plan to do, always make sure that you have *Skin in the Game* and that it really matters to you.

Is your motivation decreasing? Ask yourself: Do I have enough Skin in the Game?

I regularly observe the effects this can have at my own seminars and events. Sometimes, I offer discounted tickets, or even invite someone—this is what I do for people who are at the beginning of their careers or who are going through a difficult financial phase. However, I regularly note with this group of participants that, although people start with great ambitions in the courses, it usually fails when it comes to implementation. Things go completely differently with the participants who paid the full registration fee. Here, the words are usually followed with the appropriate actions, because these people have *Skin in the Game*. They've invested a very high sum of money in themselves and have thereby greatly reinforced their personal expectations. Thus, clarity doesn't only lead to more commitment and a high impact, but ultimately, also to an increased skill in implementation.

Success Factor Number 2: Focus

Now that you've worked on your clarity, it's all about harnessing your strength and adjusting your focus, so that you can focus on what really pushes you forward and not get distracted or bogged down with the unimportant stuff. I recommend the "heaven and hell" metaphor for this. What's behind all this? Very simple: the exclusive focus on two areas. On one side is heaven, by which I mean everything that is related to your dreams, your vision, and your strategy. You could also call it working on your company or your life. To create a mnemonic device for yourself, you might also try thinking of castles in the air that are so huge that there is only space high above them. Well, and then of course there's hell. By that, I mean the hard work, the doing, and the concrete implementation of the strategy you have developed in heaven. Please don't be confused by the negative meaning of the word hell, but I chose the term because it is the complete opposite of heaven. To be honest, focusing on the two-letter word that's been quoted so much—D-O—can sometimes feel a bit like hell, right? That's the notorious price we must be willing to pay. (I personally like to imagine the voice of AC/DC singer Bon Scott, who loudly shouts "I'm on a Highway to Hell," and it automatically puts me in a positive mood again.)

Success is found in heaven or in hell. Everything in between just distracts you.

The metaphor of heaven and hell can be a wonderful guide for your focus. Whatever your specific goals and objectives, always ask yourself: am I moving in heaven or in hell? In other words, from now on, use your three most important resources—time, energy, and money—only for tasks that are directly related to those two areas, either with your vision, your strategy, or the development of great ideas, or with the concrete implementation of these things. You should either delegate or leave everything found in between. You may be quite wonderfully busy with the tasks that are between heaven and hell, but the bottom line is that it's just a distraction that isn't productive and doesn't bring you closer to your goals. So adjust your focus. Your success will thank you.

Success Factor Number 3: Hard Work

I'd like to share with you three of my deepest convictions: "No pain, no gain," "Fortune favors the bold," and "Hard work always beats talent." Because I believe in nothing so much as in good, old-fashioned hard work. "But Ilja, that's really outdated, because in times of digital change, it's much more important to work smart, right?" I hear this objection regularly, and yet I stick with my statement because everyone works smart today. I do, too, by the way. It's simply the absolute basic prerequisite, and by no means a differentiating feature. And because that is the case, hard work pays off.

Work smart and hard. This rare combination automatically gives you a unique selling proposition.

So here we are at the third factor of the success formula, namely hard work. If you know what's important to you and focus your entire attention on these things, then it depends on how intensively—and especially in the long term—you work to make it happen. And not just once, but again and again. Even on days when you don't feel like it. When you're struggling with setbacks. When you would like to throw everything away. In all these situations, hard work helps you stay on top of it. One of my great idols, Arnold Schwarzenegger himself—the Terminator—put it perfectly in his famous "Six Rules of Success" speech with two legendary sentences:

"You can't climb the ladder of success with your hands in your pocket" and "While you are taking a nap, somebody else is working his butt off."

There's nothing more to add. No success without hard work. It's that easy.

Let the factors of clarity, focus, and hard work become an integral part of your attitude toward life.

These were the three factors of the success formula: Clarity. Focus. And hard work. Let these qualities become an integral part of your attitude toward life, and success will inevitably occur in all areas of your life. Naturally, this doesn't mean that it will now be easier, or that it will happen all by itself. On the contrary, you will continue to make mistakes, battle setbacks, and face defeats. But you will grow and get better at these challenges. And that is, perhaps, the greatest achievement of all. However, the more you dare, the more the whiners, know-it-alls, and grouches will crawl out of their holes. For your own personal contentment, it will be crucial that you dare to do a lot more of your own thing. And that's exactly what the next section is about.

THE ART OF CRITICAL THINKING

As an international keynote speaker, I have the great pleasure of being booked by my clients for conferences around the world. Sounds great, right? Well it is, to a degree, but of course it means that I spend a lot of time at airports and aboard a variety of planes, which admittedly is not one of my favorite pastimes. Incidentally, I love flying itself. It's the waiting and the increasing complexity of air travel that I don't like. But I make the best of it and use the many hours in the air for a very important thing that often gets left behind in the otherwise hectic everyday life: I enjoy time for myself. I read an exciting mystery book, watch a current movie in the on-board entertainment system, or just think about life itself. No incoming emails, phone calls, or any other distraction can bother me, and it's kind of like a spa for my soul. But when I look around on my many travels, most people are mainly traveling in "operation mode." They talk hectically into their mobile phones, chatting at extremely high volumes about internal company information so that everyone around them knows about the current problems in the company, and they open their laptops as soon as the trip starts so they can plow through extensive Excel tables with a fascinated obsession. But what's the reason for this? Why don't some people manage to relax a little on a forty-five-minute flight from Berlin to Frankfurt? On the one hand, I suspect that some managers consider themselves too important and have succumbed to the fatal error of thinking that the company couldn't get along without them for an hour. The other reason, however, is even more common. People simply cannot break out of their familiar routines and standard procedures. And naturally, familiar processes are important, because they give our job a certain stability and familiarity—just think about the core need for security. However, when you're trapped in your own routines, this basically positive characteristic quickly tips over into the negative. When processes and behaviors are no longer questioned, they tend to become absurd, ridiculous, and stupid.

The focus should ALWAYS be on the needs of your customers, never on internal processes.

Have you ever been annoyed when the employees of a company have completely lost sight of you as a customer, and their behavior is exclusively oriented toward internal company processes and requirements? In such cases, I always think of the ingenious title of the book by my esteemed colleague, Edgar Geffroy, who put it so beautifully in a nutshell:

"The only thing that disturbs us is the customer!"

In particular, when I think of visits to government agencies or calls to hotlines for major corporations, I spontaneously come up with hundreds of examples, but since we're on the topic of air travel, we'll just stick with that. Have you ever wondered why the on-board processes are the way they are? Why does the crew really need to explain the safety instructions every time, even though nobody listens anyway? Why should my small iPhone have the ability to disrupt the operation of a huge Airbus A380, but vice versa there are no difficulties?[35] I also wonder, every single time, where the flight attendants learned their announcements; and by that, of course I mean the mostly irrelevant content, but also especially the format. Seriously, no normal person talks so artificially and with such obvious disinterest. It's no wonder that nobody listens. The announcements from the cockpit always fall into exactly the same category. For many years, I've wondered who is really interested in the altitude you're flying at, what the outside temperature is, and where the wind is coming from at the destination airport. This information may be exciting for the captain and his copilot, but the passengers (a.k.a., the customers) have almost zero interest in it.

The answer is—as in so many other areas of life—that this is always how it's been done. At some point, a process was set in motion that is now reliably carried out by all parties involved, without anyone critically questioning it. The person performing these actions sweeps aside any question of the purpose, and goes through a metamorphosis to become a mindless worker bee. This leads to a fatal attitude—you only think in terms of internal processes, rules, and mechanisms, and completely forget the needs of your own customers.

Fortunately, there are more and more people who no longer let themselves be fobbed off with the killer argument, "We've always done it this way."

Banish the platitude "That's the way it's always been done" from your vocabulary.

People who think independently critically question the status quo and then give new meaning to the soulless process. Late one evening, I flew from Munich back home to Berlin, and suddenly the unexpected happened. The pilot checked in from the cockpit and in a perfectly normal voice announced, "Dear guests, I'd like to invite you to look out of the window. We pilots rarely experience such a starry night. It's just a beautiful sight. At this moment, you can look almost completely over the state of Brandenburg. And our passengers on the left side are particularly lucky, because the view as we head straight for Berlin is simply breathtaking. It fascinates me every time. I just wanted to quickly share that with you. I wish you a nice flight. Thank you for letting my team and I take you safely to your destination today."

How often do you experience situations where you want to spontaneously applaud? Fortunately, after we landed, the pilot stood in front of his cockpit so that I (and many other guests) could shake his hand and say thank you on our way off the plane. Because, even if it was only a few sentences, the deviation from the stupid (and in my eyes meaningless) routine led us to experience one of those magical moments that we like to remember for a long time. And when you look closely, your whole life is filled with these kinds of people. Unfortunately, however, we've become too accustomed to the fact that the majority of people prefer to act according to the book and leave their thinking to regulations and pointless rules. Another important element of success is critical thinking—a skill that has, unfortunately, become very rare, because many people have become used to the fact that the media, politics, or anonymous bodies tell them what is important, right, or wrong. Never succumb to this fatal convenience, but cultivate the art of critical thinking. And by that I don't mean that you should become one of those kind of people who are fundamentally against everything. No, critical thinking is—above all—the questioning of purpose, relevance, or customer orientation. My advice: question everything. Meaningless processes, internal procedures, and stupid routines. Question entrenched opinions, convictions, and prejudices—especially your own, of course.

Question everything, including this instruction that you should question everything.

Two things will happen once you start to make a difference as a critical thinker. On the one hand, you will get a lot of resistance from those around you. No wonder, because you're suddenly questioning processes, routines, and procedures that are regarded as generally accepted. That's not always pleasant, but what's the alternative? Then, something else will happen, as well. You'll notice a dramatic increase in fulfillment, satisfaction, and importance in your daily life, because you only do things that really make sense and clearly reject all pointless activities. To make it even easier for you in the future, I'd like to introduce three concrete tools to help you cultivate critical thinking.

Critical Thinking Tool #1: The Question of Sense of Purpose

The best guide we have in life is a sense of purpose. This gives meaning to an ordinary job, a reason for being to a routine, and significance to our lives. As a side note, something can be sensible or have a sense of purpose, but the widely used phrase "That makes sense" is senseless. This is yet another example of something that is used by everyone and then no longer critically questioned by anyone.

Always ask yourself: "How do I know that?"

Now we come to the crucial question, with which you can reliably test the opinions, prejudices, values, convictions, and alleged facts about your environment and, of course, also of yourself. The question is: *How do I know that?* In order to be able to answer that question, you force yourself to penetrate to the core of your original experience, and thereby to verify the meaning. The more often you ask yourself this question, the more you will notice how many opinions and convictions we have simply adopted from other people, the media, or our environment. On the one hand, this requires courage, of course, but on the other hand, it is the only way to lead a self-determined life based on your own standards.

Critical Thinking Tool #2: Create a Not-to-Do List

Yes, you read that correctly. Immediately and deliberately create a list of things that you will no longer do. Because isn't that correct? A classic to-do list often takes on gigantic dimensions, and we often simply feel overwhelmed by the mass of obligations. Fortunately, there's an extremely effective antidote to this: setting priorities and consistently saying no. No to time-killers. No to squandering. No to all the tasks we gladly deal with day in and day out, but which ultimately don't bring us even one inch closer to our goals. Remember that I mentioned this in Chapter 4: the more you cultivate the ability to say no, the more you say yes at the same time. Yes to more personal freedom. Yes to more focus.

Yes to more self-determination. So grab your journal or a piece of paper and then write down all the things you won't do from now on. Within days, you'll see how your time management becomes more effective and productive. And, as a nice side effect, creating your not-to-do list also increases your level of inner clarity at the same time.

Critical Thinking Tool #3: Create an IDGAF List

And now comes the next list, which really has it all. Similar to its big sister—the not-to-do list—the IDGAF list also focuses on letting go, saying *no*, and differentiating oneself. However, its effect is even more powerful. Of course, the name is also a bit cooler, because IDGAF stands for "I don't give a fuck!" It is precisely this attitude that is indispensable if you want to lead a self-determined life. Because the more you do your thing, the more you will experience the following reactions from those around you: incomprehension, criticism, rejection, know-it-all-ism, nagging, active opposition, and—very often—subtle emotional blackmail. You'll hear sentences like, "You can't just…", "But you should…" or "You must urgently…" Do those look familiar?

With the IDGAF list, you liberate yourself from the expectations of other people.

On the one hand, you can be a little proud when you get these kinds of reactions to your personality, because people can only grate and rub themselves against sharp corners and edges. On the other hand, however, it can also become a real burden if the resistance becomes too strong. That makes it all the more important to detach yourself from what other people think of you, expect of you, or demand of you regarding how you should function. You can't prevent all this, but you can make the decision that from now on, you don't care anymore. From now on, therefore, follow the mantra of bestselling author Tommy Jaud, who put it so wonderfully in a nutshell: "Like hell I do!" So create your own personal IDGAF list. Write down everything you don't give a fuck about: whether your life, your opinions, your decisions, or your ideas suit other people. How your clothing is received, what they say about your driving style or your musical taste. All the many things that make you say to yourself, "I don't give a fuck! As long as it makes me happy, I don't care what other people think." The more you liberate yourself from the expectations of others in this way, the more you can orient yourself toward your own standards.

With these three tools, you can take your critical thinking to a new level. It's best to hang both of these lists in a clearly visible place in your work space so that you can follow them every day. And then enjoy your life as a critical thinker. You may seem exotic to other people in an age of egalitarianism, uniformity, and mediocrity, but it's the only way to lead a fulfilled and happy life. Well, and of course you should immediately subject this assertion to a critical examination.

IT IS NEVER TOO LATE TO MAKE A BIG DIFFERENCE

I will never forget how hard I had to fight for my first paid speech. For over a year, I had positioned myself, contacted agencies, and called potential customers, without any results. You can't imagine how often I heard the word *no*, in all its conceivable variations, during that time. It's pretty amazing how many ways a single word can be pronounced—I've heard them all. Until one day, I received a call from the HR manager of a large company, whom I had probably already contacted seven times. At first, I thought she would kindly ask me not to bother her any longer, but she actually said, "Mr. Grzeskowitz, it was hard work, but I finally managed to convince our board. We'd like to book you for our annual staff event. Do you have time in early September?" On the outside, I answered, "One moment, please. I'll have to check my calendar first," which at that point brightly shone white because there were so many gaps in it. But at the same time, I did the "Klopp Saw" and pumped my fists in the air like Liverpool coach Jürgen Klopp and celebrated with an internal cheer marked by euphoria, relief, and pride.

But as soon as I hung up the phone, my endorphin rush immediately turned into extreme nervousness. No wonder, because it was quite a big event. The biggest hall in the city was chosen as the location, I was announced on two glossy pages in the company newspaper, and the

CEO personally picked me up from the train station in his car. After the previous speakers got the atmosphere simmering, all the lights were on me, and I looked into six hundred pairs of eyes that were eagerly awaiting my performance. And then it was time. The host introduced me, "Ladies and gentlemen, please welcome with me the star guest for today, the experienced top speaker and change expert, Ilja Grzeskowitz." Then I went onto the stage, took a deep breath, and proceeded to give a speech that would not have been good enough even for the parents' meeting at my daughter's kindergarten. The applause was worse than poor, the atmosphere had sunk into the basement, and I had to look into questioning faces. It's no surprise, since I now know that I had packed far too much information into my forty-five minutes, so the listeners had no choice but to be confused. The HR manager, who had campaigned so hard for me, came to me afterwards in dismay and said, "You know, Mr. Grzeskowitz, we've been holding this event for eleven years. But the mood has never been this bad. Our boss left very early."

I don't know why, but my first thought was: *How will I get back to the train station?* However, immediately afterwards, I realized what had happened. It was my big day, the performance I had been waiting for so long, the unique chance to prove myself, and I had completely screwed it up. At that moment, my dream burst like a soap bubble. I saw myself at the end of my career as a professional speaker, even though it hadn't even really started yet. I had thoughts like, "I'm sure they'll hang a big picture of me in the company headquarters with the label 'Worst Speaker Ever,'" "Nobody will ever book me again," and "I'd better go back to my old job as a department store manager, at least I can do that." I bathed in my self-pity and was actually about to drown in it. But then life gave me a helping hand, because a few days later, something happened that saved me. I was holding a seminar in Switzerland when my assistant whispered in my ear as I was setting up, "Hey Ilja, there's an elderly lady waiting for you at the reception. She'd like to speak with you." A minute later, I was looking into the brown eyes of a woman who must have been about seventy-five years old. I was more than impressed that personal development was still such a high priority for a woman of that age, but I was wrong. She actually said to me, "My father is waiting outside. He is ninety-six years old and would like to attend your seminar."

It's never too late to make a big difference!

At that precise moment, an elegant gentleman in a wheelchair comes around the corner. He wears a perfectly fitted suit, a matching tie, and under his arm he holds an ancient but very well-kept briefcase. He stretches out his hand very naturally and says loudly, "Here I am." And afterwards, a little more quietly, "I wanted to come to the last event, but my daughter is always so worried about me and canceled my participation. So I just signed up again yesterday. And secretly." Isn't that impressive? Don't you know people who, at the age of twenty, think that by the end of school they will have learned and already know everything that life has to offer? While I'm standing there shaking the hand of a man who still wants to learn at almost one hundred years of age. At the same time, my self-confidence is still pretty shattered, so I answer, "It's a great honor for me to welcome you to my seminar, but what can I teach you that you don't already know?" And he looks at me with a keen eye and says, "Ilya, don't make yourself smaller than you are. I've read your books and they're great. I just want to go deeper into the subject of change. I am the chairman of two associations, publisher of a magazine, and am currently writing a book. I still have so many dreams I want to fulfill. The time I have may be limited, but one thing I know for sure is—it's never too late to make a big difference!"

Please, how cool is that? It's never too late to make a big difference. Have you also come across sentences like this that stick in your head the first time you hear them? That's exactly how it was for me. This one sentence not only shook my life to its foundations, but it also saved my career. If a ninety-six-year-old man goes through life with the attitude that his best time is not behind but ahead of him, if he radiates so much optimism and confidence, if he has so much desire for change, why on earth am I even wasting a single thought on giving up? At that moment, I swore to fight for my dream and make a difference, too. I've worked harder than ever before—like a man possessed—on my books, and I've given as many lectures as I could. And if there was another setback—and there were a lot of those, because if you act a lot, you make a lot of mistakes—then I asked myself the following questions: "What can I learn from this?", "How can I do it better?", and "How do I have to change?"

Since then, I've published seven more books and lectured in fifteen countries on four continents. And the most important thing is that more than half of my bookings as a keynote speaker today come from the personal recommendations of satisfied and enthusiastic customers. That's what I'm most proud of. But even though I'm very grateful for this, it's all just a commitment to work on my vision, to keep changing, and to grow as a person every day.

Thanks to meeting this wonderful gentleman, I know that it's never too late to make a big difference, and that the strongest motivation often springs from our hardest moments.

That is probably my greatest lesson learned from this experience. That we are never the best when the sun is shining, but instead when the wind is really blowing directly into our faces. That every problem always offers a chance to develop a deep motivation from it. That we should never give up, because defeats only make us stronger. You don't really believe that? Then let me give you a few examples of how to use problems to motivate yourself.

- Someone says to you, "You'll never make it," and then you think, "I'll show you," and then you just do it.
- Are you experiencing a severe setback? So what! Think: Now more than ever!
- You hear the statement, "That's impossible." The following thought develops in your mind: "Wrong! So far, nobody has found a way that it could work, and I'm going to look for it."
- You are once again "too..." for somebody. Remember? "Too fat, too thin, too old, too young, too inexperienced, too big, too small..." Your reaction? "Think what you want. I'll succeed without your permission."
- Does an unsolved problem in your company frustrate you simply because no one addresses it? You quit, start your own business, and replace your old employer as the market leader.
- Someone says, "You can't do that." You respond, "Wanna bet?"

- Someone slings at you, "Can't you be satisfied for once?" And you know that, deep inside, you are extremely satisfied, but you are never satisfied with the status quo, because life consists of growth and development.

Do you see what I mean? I hope that you will never forget the following two things:

1. Whenever other people criticize you, tell you something, or want to keep you down, these contemporaries are not really talking to you. They are talking to themselves and, in reality, criticizing themselves, explaining to themselves why they think something is not working, and repeating their own limiting beliefs, which then intensify over time.
2. The "now more than ever" mentality gives rise to a deep inner motivation that not only has a high intensity, but also lasts particularly long. So don't be angry the next time you fail spectacularly, suffer a painful defeat, or deal with fierce resistance from those around you. These situations are only negative at first glance. Over the long term, they are the source of courage, a strong drive, and the decisive commitment that will ensure that your personal definition of success will become a reality.

If you have any doubts, think of the words of wisdom from Ralph Waldo Emerson, who so wonderfully pointed out, "From the ruins of our despair, we build our character." How right he was. After all, it is never too late to make a difference.

Changemaker's Memo: The Five Big Ideas from This Chapter

1. The question that can change your life is, "What does success mean to me?"
2. The three most important success factors are: Clarity, Focus, Hard Work.
3. Question everything: meaningless processes, internal procedures, and stupid routines, as well as generally accepted opinions, convictions, and prejudices.
4. It is never too late to make a difference.
5. Every problem offers a great opportunity to develop a deep motivation from it.

CHAPTER 9

The "Smells Like Teen Spirit" Rule for a Fulfilling Life

With the lights out, it's less dangerous,
here we are now, entertain us.
I feel stupid and contagious,
here we are now, entertain us.

—Nirvana, "Smells Like Teen Spirit"

I had never thought that a single push of a button could turn life completely upside down. Yet, that's exactly what happened to me in the fall of 1991. At the age of sixteen, I had reached the height of my adolescent rebellion, so it was not surprising that I responded with a curt, "No. No way," to my parents' question of whether I would come along with them on a family holiday. And so it happened that, for the first time in my life, I would be responsible for myself for two whole weeks. In my mind's eye, I could already envision the coming time. Hours of rehearsing with my band, greasy food from the pizza delivery service, and regular parties with my buddies. (I don't want to mention here without a certain pride that we always had a high surplus of girls at our parties. And that's without Tinder, PickUp, and flirty videos on YouTube. Take that, Generation App-Dependent!)

My first official act as a temporary bachelor in my parental row house was to connect the TV to my hi-fi tower in order to provide the needed perpetual sound of loud rock music. (For the younger readers, a hi-fi was a combination of record, cassette, and CD player.) And that's when it happened. I switched on the channel that I used at that time as a kind of twenty-four-hour continuous sound system: MTV (Music Television). The guitar riff that sounded through the speakers a short time later hit me like a steam hammer. It was the famous beginning to Nirvana's song "Smells Like Teen Spirit." Hypnotized, I stared at the TV for the next five minutes and instinctively felt that I was witnessing something extraordinary. With their energetic grunge sound, the band had revolutionized the music world overnight. Nirvana managed to put their personal stamp on music in a way that, before, only Elvis, the Beatles, or Michael Jackson had done. Nothing would be the same after that, and to date, their album *Nevermind*, featuring the song "Smells Like Teen Spirit," has sold over twenty-six million copies.

There are moments of fate in which the fundamental course of the future is set.

In retrospect, I am more than grateful that I was able to experience this milestone in music history up close. (I'm sometimes a little sorry for today's youth, who have to grow up with mainstream artists like Justin Bieber, David Guetta, or Miley Cyrus. Well, not really.) Together with the fall of the Berlin Wall, 9/11, and the birth of my two daughters, it is one of the most emotionally intense moments of my life. I remember exactly how we all wanted to be like singer Kurt Cobain back then. We started wearing the baggy look, grew our hair out, and imitated his style of playing the guitar. If that angry young man from Aberdeen, Washington, could make it, so could we. His story fascinated us, because he lived the exact life we all dreamed of. Coming from a humble background, he quickly became *the* megastar of the 1990s. He toured the whole world, lived off his music, and people laid themselves at his feet. With Courtney Love, he had a beautiful woman at his side, and together they had a daughter, Francis Bean. Everything seemed perfect and the hype around Kurt Cobain knew no bounds—until the singer put a shotgun in his mouth on April 5, 1994, and killed himself. He was only twenty-seven years old. His farewell letter ended with a line from the Neil Young song, "Hey Hey, My My": *It's better to burn out, than to fade away.*

I will probably never forget how an entire generation shed a flood of tears together around the death of this exceptional musician. And for me, personally, a very specific question arose that simply would not let go of me: how could a person who had achieved everything the rest of the world dreamed of voluntarily take his life? It was one of those fateful moments that probably set the fundamental course for the future, because, for the first time in my life, I realized how grateful I could be. For the people in my life, for the external circumstances in which I grew up, and for my life itself, which I enjoyed to the fullest then. I have kept this gratitude until today. It helps me to go through life with a certain humility and to never lose my grounding in everything I do. But that's not all, because Kurt Cobain's death taught me three important lessons that influenced and molded my personality. I call them my "Smells Like Teen Spirit" Rules for a fulfilled life:

SLTSR #1: Don't Fake It 'til You Make It

The life of the Nirvana singer is a prime example of what can happen if you follow other people's definition of success. If you lead a life that isn't your own. If you put a good face on the outside and are helplessly dissatisfied on the inside. Therefore, take off your mask and always be yourself.

SLTSR #2: Don't Waste Your Time with Negativity

Life is precious and often flies by faster than we can imagine. So don't waste it whining and doubting or worrying about trivialities. Here's how I see it: five minutes of whining is okay. When I get angry about something, I take the liberty of letting out my feelings for the duration of "Smells Like Teen Spirit"—which, by the way, is exactly five minutes and two seconds long—giving in to my frustration and possibly even bathing in self-pity. But after that, I immediately stop and focus again on solutions, possibilities, and the beautiful things in life.

SLTSR #3: Enjoy the Growth Staircase

Life is growth, and every stage of development has its magical moments. As much as I believe in a grateful look back and courageous plans for the future, it's even more important to enjoy the moments along the way, and in that way, to give meaning to every single step on the Growth Staircase. Surrendering yourself to each moment, from your head to your toes, and not hoping for shortcuts, miraculous formulas, or lost secrets. To accept that mistakes and setbacks are not negative things, but indispensable factors for long-term happiness and deep satisfaction.

These are my three "Smells Like Teen Spirit" Rules, which have been my faithful companions for years. I hope they will also be that for you in your everyday life. We want to use them as a central theme in this chapter, to perhaps take the most important step in this book—on the way to your true and genuine personality. And who knows, you may also have the chorus of "Smells Like Teen Spirit" in your ear as you look at your life with gratitude and take nothing—nothing at all—for granted: your health, the people around you, or the fact that you have enough food on the table every day. All these things are wonderful gifts in life that we should rejoice in every single day.[36] Don't you agree?

With the lights out, it's less dangerous. Here we are now, entertain us. I feel stupid and contagious. Here we are now, entertain us.

DON'T FAKE IT 'TIL YOU MAKE IT

Fake it 'til you make it! Have you ever heard that phrase before? Whenever I stumble upon this statement, I get a rash, because I think this advice is the most fatal thing you can give a person. For many years, I've not only fought against this sentence, but also for more. More genuineness. More vulnerability. More humanity. One encounter had a particular influence on me. "Ilja, come a little closer." My grandmother wasn't doing too well that day. She had just celebrated her ninety-fourth birthday and had been living in a nursing home for dementia patients for two years. She used to be a beautiful woman, but today, after years of physical and mental decay, she sits in a wheelchair and forgets just about everything. There are days when she no longer even recognizes her own family. But on that day, she had one of her few clear moments when it was perfectly normal to talk to her. She even had a little smile on her face, when she said, "Ilja, all my life I have been guided by the expectations of others. When I was young, I had so many dreams. But I always played it safe, did what everyone else did, and waited for the perfect moment. However, that moment has never come. There was always something that seemed more important. And now it's too late. I am so proud of you, because you're living the life I always dreamed of. You live a life that is oriented toward your expectations, your values, and your dreams."

Then she pressed a gold pocket watch into my hand and said, "This is my beloved watch. I don't need it anymore, and I hope it will find a good use with you. It should always remind you that our time here on earth is limited." I admit it, I was wondering if I should point out to her that pocket watches had gone a bit out of fashion. But I swallowed that thought and instead said, "Thank you, Grandma, I love you!" A few minutes later, she had disappeared back into her very own world, and tears shot into my eyes. For as much as I would have liked to believe her words, she was unfortunately completely wrong. Of course, from the outside, I was quite successful. I always knew what I wanted, and being a writer and keynote speaker had always been my dream. But internally, I was unhappy and struggled against myself, because far too often, I was anxious to please other people and to play a role that was not in harmony with my inner core. I wasn't myself. I wasn't genuine. Instead, I was always in business mode, trying to look as perfect as possible, forgetting to be myself.

Avoid representing something that you are not. Be yourself.

And here we come to the famous advice, *Fake it 'til you make it*. Let me reiterate this point clearly. That sentence is pretty much the biggest bullshit I've ever heard. (I've considered for a long time whether the word *bullshit* can be used in a business book. But it's my book, after all, and that's where I will apply my rules.) I can say that so emphatically, because I myself had followed this model for far too long. But if there's one thing I could wish for, it would be for you to forget this advice as soon as possible. "Wait a minute, Ilja. I've been to several seminars over the past year and have read many books where the exact opposite was said. *Fake it 'til you make it* was stressed as a basic requirement for success!" Believe me, I know that objection. And yet, I stick to my statement, because on the one hand, a sentence doesn't become any truer just because it is repeated constantly and perpetually. Nor does the relevance increase if everyone does it. Incidentally, this is a widespread phenomenon in the continuing education scene. Hardly anyone communicates their own thoughts and opinions anymore, but they limit themselves to babbling on and communicating what they heard somewhere else. I gladly recommend a high dose of critical thinking. The second reason, however, is even more decisive. The content of this old motivational drivel is simply wrong. It erroneously neglects to ask the important question of how the person you would like to become would behave. No, this sentence simply encourages you to fool yourself and the people around you. To represent something you're not. To play far too big a role just to gain recognition and acceptance.

Fake it 'til you make it is the biggest nonsense you can recommend to a person.

But why do so many people follow this advice? The reason for this is simply fear. Fear of being rejected, unwanted, or unloved. Fear of doing something wrong, not being perfect, or not complying with a certain social norm. Fear of being the person you really are. But that's exactly the point. To dare to be real. But instead, most people hide behind earnest, serious, and—especially—uncomfortable masks. You show a certain behavior, because that's what one does. It's better to act with your customers, employees, and colleagues than to have the courage to carry your true core to the outside world. And that is tragic, because this strategy never leads to the desired result. Why, you ask? Very simply, nobody likes a fake. People like people. With all their strengths, but also their weaknesses. They don't expect you to be perfect. Quite the opposite. All they want is for you to be yourself. They want you to be real. Listen to your heart, feel inside yourself, and trust your own opinion more than the expectations of society. Sooner or later, you'll discover the people behind all the masks we love to wear. And from that day on, you have only one task in your life: to express your unique personality with every fiber of your being. Verbally and nonverbally. In your job and at home. If you have the courage, a deep sense of fulfillment will come with it.

I know exactly what I'm talking about. After talking with my grandmother, I made a promise to myself that's probably been the biggest booster of my career. It has brought me more customers, more money, and more orders than all the tips and tricks of the supposed experts put together. I gave myself my word never to wear a false and uncomfortable mask again, but to express my real personality in all my thoughts and actions. To accept my weaknesses and let the world see that I'm not perfect. Every time I doubt this decision, I take my grandmother's pocket watch out of its drawer. It reliably reminds me that I am good enough as I am, and that it's much more important to know what matters most to me than to be guided by what other people expect from me. And since then, I follow my new mantra: *Don't fake it 'til you make it!*

Just be real instead. Because real is always good enough.

You are not in this world to be perfect. You are in this world to be real.

Here's one more important lesson I learned from my grandmother. During this time, her roommates in the nursing home changed three times. One thing was the same for each of them: photos of loved ones stood on the little bedside table. They weren't photos of expensive cars, luxurious handbags, or 3D TVs. They were wives, husbands, children, and siblings. Because when life enters its final phase, many people remember what really counts and what is truly important. Often, they look back wistfully and regret not having taken enough risks, not having lived intensively enough, and not having dared anything extraordinary. With an intense longing, you think of the many unfulfilled dreams, missed opportunities, and days wasted with trivialities. And then you're frustrated—about yourself, the lifestyle oriented toward the expectations of others, and your own passivity. About the fact that you worked far too often and were a conforming sheep in the large herd. Would you agree with me? Really, no one thinks on their deathbed: "I wish I'd spent more time at the office."

It's our task in life to express our unique personality with every fiber of our being.

At the end of this section, I'd like to inspire you with a crazy idea: die every day and wake up in the morning aware that your time on this beautiful earth is finite. Nobody gets out of here alive. And this is by no means one of those cuddly motivational phrases, but a reminder to shape every single day of your life as if it were the last. To pull your dreams out of their drawer and start implementing them. Live as intensely as if there were no tomorrow. Laugh. Love. Learn to appreciate the things we take for granted so often. Because in order to enjoy your life to the fullest, you don't need any strokes of fate, illnesses, or near-death experiences. And if another day is given to you on this wonderful earth, then do it again tomorrow. But please don't forget to go the extra mile.

Die every day and be grateful for the supposedly small things that we take for granted far too often.

DON'T WASTE YOUR TIME ON NEGATIVITY

Let's come now to the ruthless truth about one of the most important—but at the same time, most controversial—topics. I'm talking about positive thinking. Some have subjected themselves unconditionally to this philosophy, while others condemn it completely and dismiss it as esoteric humbug. This, of course, has a corresponding impact. While the followers of the first variant—with a permanent grin on their face, rose-colored glasses over their eyes, and naive trust—simply ignore and smile away any problem, the opponents of positive thinking often become cynics whose glasses are half empty, whose skies are full of dark clouds, and whose everyday lives are usually quite dull. It's obvious that both strategies are unsuitable for leading a content life. Nevertheless, I keep hearing the question, "Is positive thinking good or bad now?" Forgive me if I don't give a direct answer, but I'd like to draw your attention to a very common pitfall that can be seen here in its purest form:

If the question is wrong, the answer doesn't matter.

That is exactly the case here. The question has a misleading focus and sets its attention on only one aspect of the big picture, namely the thinking. But at the same time, one ignores the other important factors: the actions, the habits, and the general mindset with which one approaches life with all its tasks. That is what this is all about—the fundamental approach. And as for that, I have a very clear opinion: don't waste your life on negativity, but be positive. Always. The latest knowledge, the best skills, and the most modern techniques are of no use to you if you impugn your everyday life with a negative attitude. Conversely, this doesn't mean that you will automatically be successful with a positive mindset. No. An inner attitude based on opportunities and possibilities alone doesn't allow you to achieve anything at all. But you can achieve everything better with a positive attitude than with a negative attitude. For over fifteen years, I've been studying human behavior in all its facets. And not even once have I met someone who would have achieved positive results with a negative focus. You are welcome to put this to the test. Take a look at those around you. I'll bet that you won't find a successful person whose DNA is encoded for negativity.

A negative mindset and positive results are mutually exclusive.

So don't waste your time with negativity, but concentrate on the numerous opportunities and possibilities. This doesn't mean that problems are disregarded, risks aren't identified, or other challenges are ignored. On the contrary. The trick is to recognize these situations and, at the same time, think in terms of possible solutions. The focus of your internal patterns of thought is crucial. The quality of our attitude determines the quality of our results. But what does this look like for you? Over the last few years, in my seminars and coaching sessions, I've compiled a list of the questions I hear over and over again. Would you like a little taste? Here are my Top Ten:

The TOP TEN Problem-Oriented Questions

1. Why does this always happen to me?
2. Why can't I succeed?
3. Why doesn't anybody in the company like me?
4. Why can't I find my vision?
5. Why does everything work out for everyone else but me?
6. Why am I unable to achieve my goals?
7. Why do I fail every time something happens?
8. Why do I magically attract problems?
9. Why me of all people?
10. Why is change so difficult?

Do any of these look familiar? These questions have one thing in common: they are pointless, because they are backward-facing and problem-oriented. As Albert Einstein aptly stated, "Problems cannot be solved with the same mindset that created them." If you ask yourself solution-oriented questions instead, you'll immediately see a massive shift in your focus. Here, too, I've prepared a Top Ten list for you:

The TOP TEN Solution-Oriented Questions

1. How can I solve this situation?
2. What can I learn from it?
3. Who could support or help me?
4. When have I ever faced a similar situation?
5. What can I learn from it?
6. What are the resources I need to reach XYZ?
7. What could a solution to the problem look like?
8. How must I change in order to reach the goal?
9. Which opportunities lurk in this challenge?
10. How must I think differently in order to achieve the goal?

That's the small, but subtle, distinction that makes a difference. These positive questions are inevitably followed by positive actions, resulting in positive results. A self-reinforcing spiral of success emerges that, over the course of time, deeply anchors itself in your subconscious and reliably does its service there. Of course, even with the most positive mindset, there will still be situations that annoy you, frustrate you, or drive you crazy. Wonderful. Always remember:

Five minutes of whining is okay!

After that, the motto is: positive focus on solutions and possibilities. Because life is just too beautiful to be squandered on negativity. Enjoy every single moment and transform the supposedly big problems into opportunities at least as big. Your most important ally—next to your mindset—is, by the way, a factor you like to forget called humor. Yes, you read that right. Because humor opens the door to every single change. Not just for the small challenges of everyday life, but also for the truly big obstacles. Really, every successful person I know likes to laugh—and a lot—especially about himself. Only those who don't take themselves too seriously can be taken seriously by those around them. Nobody likes bitter, always serious, and stony contemporaries. After all, these people don't like themselves very much. The great art is to tackle the supposedly small tasks with great seriousness and laugh at the difficult, seemingly insurmountable, and often frustrating challenges. I would like to conclude this section with the golden rules of a positive mindset:

The Three Golden Rules of a Positive Mindset

1. Be positive. Always.
2. Perceive problems, but at the same time, think of opportunities and possibilities.
3. Humor opens the door to change. Laugh a lot, and often, and don't take yourself too seriously.

Wonderful things will happen if you let these three rules become your daily companions from now on.

ENJOY THE GROWTH STAIRCASE

In my seminars, coaching sessions, and consultations, I almost always ask my clients this question: "What is your main goal for the next twelve months?"[37] The answer I hear as often as any other breaks my heart every time: "I want to be happy and content." You ask, what's wrong with that? Of course, it's not the wish in and of itself, because what could be better than to experience real happiness and a deep contentment? The tragedy of this supposed goal is something completely different. It's the assumption that happiness and contentment are conditions that would depend on external factors. The internal pattern originates from the following procedure: once I have reached my goal (I have finished my studies, completed further training, have been promoted, moved, bought a new car, founded my company, become a mother, etc.), then I can finally be happy and content. Do you recognize the error in this reasoning? Happiness and contentment never depend on external circumstances. These conditions cannot be bought, they do not arise over time, and they do not fall from the sky over the course of time. If you keep just one thing from this book, it would fill my heart with joy if it were this sentence:

Happiness and contentment are a decision we have to make anew every day.

Have I shaken your beliefs too much with this sentence? If so, then I'm glad. Because if you are one of those people whose main goal is to be happy and content, then it's time for a rethink. Let me repeat: happiness and contentment are a decision that you have to make anew every day. These states of mind don't arise at some point from any external events, but they arise deep inside of you, through your choices to be grateful, enjoy the little things in life, and enjoy every single moment. Do you want to be happy? Wonderful, then be happy. And not in twelve months, but today. Now. Right away. Do you want to lead a content life? Then make the decision to do it. Where you are right now, with the external circumstances that are currently prevailing. Don't wait for *sometime*, because it's almost always a *never*.

And now we are in the middle of the final—but possibly also the most important—section of this book. I spent a long time wondering if it would have been better to put this content closer to the front of the book, but ultimately decided against it. For one thing, the things that you read at the end of a book are remembered much better than those in the middle section (remember the dodos, battery changers, and the full bank accounts?). And another thing—it was important for me to first familiarize you with the basics necessary for a complete understanding. I didn't want to take the fourth step before taking the first. Now we are arriving at a model that has shaken up my business, my daily life, and my way of living, and hopefully it will trigger the same effect on you.. I'm talking about the Growth Staircase, which I have visualized in the following illustration.

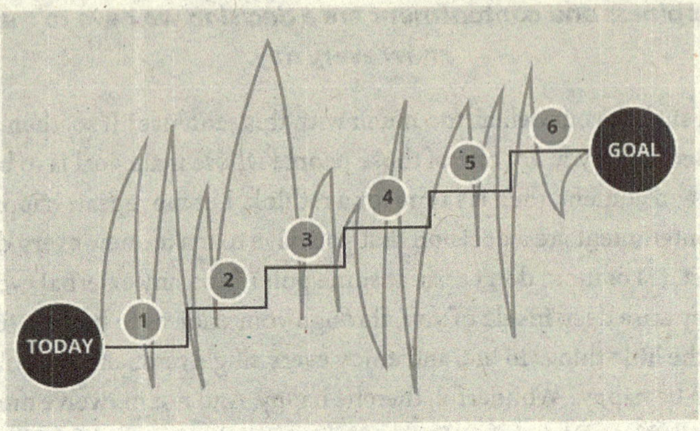

The Growth Staircase

Life is not a straight line, but a fast roller-coaster ride with ups and downs, successes and defeats.

The idea behind it is very simple. The lower left circle represents the status quo, the person you are today, and the life you are currently leading. The upper right circle symbolizes your future, your visions, and represents the personality you want to be in the future. Already we can see the big mistake that many people fall for in their way of thinking: the assumption that the road between today and our goal would be a straight line. But that's simply not the way life works. Rather, it's more of a rapid roller-coaster ride with ups and downs, successes and defeats, rapid changes in direction, steep climbs, adrenaline-producing loops, but above all—a huge amount of fun. I tried to visualize this wild ride via a zigzag line. In reality, it would look even more complex—more like a mighty ball of yarn. After all, we often have to overcome obstacles, take a new approach, or deal with failures along our way. Do you agree?

But that's not all. Within the zigzag line, a very special process arises, which we have often described in this book using the term *personality development*. This runs in steps, which I have titled in the illustration with circles numbered from one to six. The idea behind it is that, over time, we go through different developmental phases that reflect our current state of knowledge, skills, experiences, and insights. Each individual step has its own unique features and very special educational tasks. Once we have mastered these, we grow as human beings and climb to the next personality step, on which we then have to master the next educational tasks. Until we finally reach our destination or, along the way, we recognize that another goal is much more attractive or relevant.

Whatever you want to achieve in life—with every goal, vision, and dream—the Growth Staircase is waiting to be climbed by you. I know what's on your mind now. No, there are no shortcuts, no elevator, or any other way to more quickly get to the upper right circle. And that's a good thing, because every single step is a milestone that is worth enjoying and savoring intensely. Above all, however, you must master the challenges in order to be able to tackle the next stage of your personal development. That's why it's not worthwhile to compare yourself to people who've been where you want to be for ten years. These people are many steps ahead of you, and you must first complete them successfully. These people struggle with their own educational tasks and challenges.

Now it should be very clear again why the sentence *Fake it 'til you make it* is such nonsense. Because what good is it to pretend that you're already on the sixth step, when you're currently busy mastering the objectives on the first? Enjoy your current state of development; be happy that the path itself is the real goal. Each step has its positive and negative characteristics. At each step, there are people who come into your life, while others leave it. And at each step, fate gives you tasks to master. Then, on the next step, the game starts again from the beginning. It stays true to the adage:

As soon as you find the answer, life changes the question.

And almost imperceptibly, the circle of thoughts that we opened at the beginning of the book closes. Because in times of perpetual change, increasing complexity, and constant uncertainty, a radically human approach—with full concentration on personality as a success factor—will be the key to a life full of self-determination, personal breakthroughs, and fulfilling freedom. It doesn't matter where you are today. As long as you are ready to climb the Growth Staircase step by step and enjoy the resulting roller-coaster ride, you are more than prepared for the challenges of the coming years. I can't tell you exactly what the future will look like, but I've decided to put the stamp of my personality on it and to actively shape it. And it is radically human. To paraphrase a well-known saying, "The one waits for the perfect moment. The other takes the moment and makes it perfect." I made my decision many years ago. Which do you choose?

Changemaker's Memo: The Five Big Ideas from This Chapter

1. Don't fake it 'til you make it. You are not in this world to be perfect, you are in this world to be real.
2. Die daily and be grateful for the supposedly small things that we take for granted far too often.
3. A negative mindset and positive results are mutually exclusive.
4. Five minutes of whining is okay! And then focus your full power back on a potential solution.
5. Enjoy every single step on the Growth Staircase.

OUTRO

Be the Change

I am in love with a girl called Annie Idea.
Annie you told me you lost your heart at high school.
Is it your next rebellion? What you want is desperation.
No idea—is death for you!
Annie flies the lovebomber, the lovebomber, yeah yeah.

—Phillip Boa and the Voodoo Club, "Annie Flies the Lovebomber"

Many years ago, a woman and her husband went to a guru in the mountains of Nepal to get some advice. They had had to wait months for the appointment, so they were very excited when they finally faced the wise man with the miraculous powers. "What can I do for you, my child?" the guru asked. The woman cleared her throat and then answered in a meek voice, "My husband is a heavy smoker and just can't get rid of his vice. It's extremely harmful to his health, and I've already tried everything. You are our last hope, and the journey from our little village took three whole days. I know that he would listen to you, because you are a great role model for him." The guru listened attentively, nodded a few times and then said, "I understand. Come back in two weeks." The woman was a bit taken aback, but she and her husband set off on their way. When the couple returned after two weeks as arranged, the guru was waiting for them. He let the husband step forward and then said calmly, but firmly, "My son, stop smoking. It is not good for you and harms your health." The woman waited a few seconds for further words from the guru, but nothing more came from him. Her face reddened and she got angry. With a trembling voice, she said, "What, that's it? We undertook this arduous journey again for this? You could have given this advice to my husband two weeks ago." The guru looked at the couple sympathetically and replied, "No, my child. Because two weeks ago, I myself smoked."

Dear reader, with this little anecdote, our time together is coming to an end. At the same time, the final thought is the most important one. Because when I speak in my lectures and events about my radically human approach, I very often hear, "That sounds pretty good in theory, Ilja, but look at the world. The train for more humanity has long since left the station." Believe me, I understand objections like this. Crisis upon crisis is spreading around the globe, reports of wars, revolutions, and terrorist attacks have long been part of our everyday lives, and even in our own personal environment, the dog-eat-dog mentality seems to be gaining more and more ground. And that's not all. The oceans are filling with plastic waste, environmental pollution has reached gigantic proportions, and global warming has led to a massive increase in the frequency of natural disasters in recent years. Yes, I admit it—it's understandable to resign yourself, to become cynical, and to be afraid of the future in the face of these developments.

Yet, at this point, I would like to offer you an alternative attitude. Despite all these conditions, we live in the best of all imaginable times. Never before have the opportunities and possibilities been so vast, and the degree of personal freedom so pronounced, as in 2018. Nor do I agree with the generally prevailing lamentation that mankind is bad in and of itself. On the contrary. For me, the people—the individual personalities with all their strengths and weaknesses, with their hopes and needs, with their ideas and dreams—are always the decisive factor that makes life really worth living. I have the great privilege of speaking at conferences around the globe. Often, people from more than fifty different nations, with different religions, skin colors, and sexual orientations, come together at these events. And do you know what? For me, these days are among the most beautiful days ever. Because there is never a quarrel, only a very special atmosphere that is characterized by mutual appreciation, openness, and curiosity. For many years, I've wondered why people get along so well on a small scale, when it seems so difficult on the world political stage. Today, I realized the decisive difference. It's just a small shift in a person's attitude, but it makes a huge difference. It's the decision not to point the finger at others and not to hope that things, crises, and people will change on their own but to take on responsibility and be—themselves—the change they wish for in their lives, businesses, and society.

Be the change!

This has been my company's slogan for many years. And because more and more people are connecting with this philosophy, I'm not worried about the future at all. On the contrary, I look forward to actively shaping it. Of course, it's much easier to convince yourself that nothing can be changed and then to hope that others will do something. It's much harder to change yourself and get things done. But in the best sense, I believe there is no alternative but to decide for the latter of these two possibilities. We must be the change we want for the world. Although this may often seem frustrating and pointless, it's the only possible way. If we do without plastic packaging from today on, it may not make any difference to the overall picture, but we can only start with ourselves. And who knows, maybe we'll inspire others to do the same. No matter what you are dissatisfied with, be the change and start changing your own world. As soon as your focus shifts in this way, you'll see how many great people are out there who are working with us to transform the world for the better.

Be the change.

And never forget one thing: the world is full of wonderful people. And if you can't find one, then just be one yourself!

The others talk. We do.

Be the change!

Sincerely yours,

Ilja Grzeskowitz

Acknowledgements

One of the most beautiful moments in an author's life is when, for the first time, you hold your own work in print in your hands. These experiences always have an almost spiritual effect on me, because they remind me of what can become of an idea that forms one day in the mind, and then—in materialized form—sees the light of day many months later. But as I mentioned in this book, even an author never wins alone, and the birth of a book is always the result of successful teamwork. I would therefore like to use this section to thank all the people who have helped make sure that you, dear reader, can now have the finished version of *The Changemaker Mindset* in your hands.

First and foremost, I would like to again the entire team of Mango Publishing as well as Kerstin Schlosser for connecting us. The next huge thank-you goes to Heinrich Kürzeder and the whole crew at my agency, Global Top Speakers. For many years now, you have been making sure that the contents of my books find their way onto the stages of this world. But despite all the joy of our joint professional success, the best thing in life is when professional relationships become personal friendships. I am very grateful for this and am already looking forward to further sales records, new lecture concepts, and—above all—cozy dumpling parties.

The next huge thank-you goes to Heinrich Kürzeder and the whole team at my agency, *Global Top Speakers*. For many years now, you have been making sure that the contents of my books find their way onto the stages of this world. But despite all the joy of our joint professional success, the best thing in life is when professional relationships become personal friendships. I am very grateful for this and am already looking forward to further sales records, new lecture concepts, and—above all—cozy dumpling parties.

What would a speaker and author be without his customers? Right, absolutely nothing. I would therefore like to thank the many companies out there who have relied on my expertise and change concepts for years and often give my books away to all their employees. (By the way, I enjoy signing books even more than writing them myself. Just a broad hint there.) I would also like to thank all my readers who have bought, given away, or recommended one (or more) of my books over the last few years. It always fills my heart with joy when I receive letters (yes, I still receive those), emails, or WhatsApps in which people tell me that one of my ideas has helped them turn their lives upside down, make radical changes, and finally live their dreams. Feedback like this is what motivates me to put all my passion into every single word, comma, and period during the gray hours of loneliness in an author's life. Thank you for your loyalty!

I thank my international speaker family for the wonderful exchanges, the always positive feedback, and the productive networking. It's simply a great feeling to have friends in almost every city around the globe. Let's make a bigger pie together.

And last but not least, my biggest thanks goes to the most important people in my life—my family. My parents Karin and Joachim. My sister Alexa, with Mette, Frida, and Pelle. My wonderful wife Silke. And especially to my two wonderful daughters, Emma and Elisabeth. You are the rock of my life and I love you.

Bibliography

Here you will find books that I have mentioned in *The Changemaker Mindset*, or which I would like to recommend to you as further, and more in-depth, reading material:

- Azzerad, Michael: *Come as You Are: The Story of Nirvana*. Broadway Books, Penguin Random House, New York 1993
- Branson, Richard: *Like a Virgin: Secrets They Won't Teach You at Business School*. Penguin Group, New York 2012
- Burchard, Brendon: *The Motivation Manifesto*. Hay House, Inc., New York 2014
- Cardone, Grant: *Be Obsessed or Be Average*. Portfolio, New York 2016
- Chomsky, Noam: *Language and Mind*. Cambridge University Press, New York 2006
- Covey, Stephen R.: *The 7 Habits of Highly Effective People. Powerful Lessons in Personal Change*. Simon & Schuster, New York 1989
- Dilts, Robert u. a.: *Beliefs: Pathways to Health and Well-Being*. Crown House Publishing Ltd., Carmarthen, United Kingdom 2012
- Drucker, Peter F.: *Management: Tasks, Responsibilities, Practices*. HarperCollins, New York 1973
- Duhigg, Charles: *The Power of Habit: Why We Do What We Do in Life and Business*. Random House, New York 2012
- Ferriss, Tim: *The 4-Hour Workweek: Escape the 9–5, Live Anywhere, and Join the New Rich*. Vermillion, Penguin Random House, New York 2010
- Hardy, Darren: *The Entrepreneur Rollercoaster: Why Now is the Time to Join the Ride*. Greenleaf Book Group, Lake Dallas 2015
- Hayzlett, Jeffrey W.: *Think Big, Act Bigger: The Rewards of Being Relentless*. Entrepreneur Press, Fitch 2015
- Heath, Chip; Heath, Dan: *Switch: How to Change Things When Change Is Hard*. Crown Publishing, New York 2010

- Holiday, Ryan: *The Ego Is the Enemy: The Fight to Master Our Greatest Opponent*. Penguin Random House, New York 2016
- Johnson, Spencer: *Who Moved My Cheese?* G.P. Putnam's Sons, New York 1998
- Kahnemann, Daniel: *Thinking, Fast and Slow*. Farrar, Straus and Giroux, New York 2011
- Keillor, Garrison: *Lake Wobegon Days*. Penguin Books, New York 1990
- Keller, Gary: *The One Thing: The Surprisingly Simple Truth Behind Extraordinary Results*. John Murray Press, London 2001
- Kotter, John: *Leading Change*. Harvard Business Review Press, Brighton, Massachusetts 2012
- Pennington, Randy: *Make Change Work*. John Wiley & Sons, Hoboken, New Jersey 2013
- Pink, Daniel H.: *Drive: The Surprising Truth About What Motivates Us*. Riverhead Books, New York 2009
- Risner, Nigel: *It's a Zoo around here*. Limitless Publications, Ross-on-Wye, UK 2002
- Robert, Cavett: *Leaving a lasting legacy*. Creative Training Techniques International, 1998
- Schwarzenegger, Arnold: *Total Recall: My Unbelievable True Life Story*. Simon & Schuster Paperbacks, New York 2012
- Simon Sinek: *Start with Why*. Portfolio, London 2013
- Strelecky, John: *The Big Five for Life*. Aspen Light Publishing, Windermere, Florida 2012
- Vaynerchuck, Gary: *#AskGaryVee: One Entrepreneur's Take on Leadership, Social Media, and Self-Awareness*. HarperCollins, New York 2016
- Wiseman, Richard: *Paranormality: Why we see what isn't there*. Spin Solutions Ltd., Hertfordshire, UK 2011
- Ziglar, Zig: *See You at the Top*. Pelican Publishing, Gretna 2000

Endnotes

1 http://www.grzeskowitz.com/clients-testimonials/

2 A detailed look into the model can be found, for example, here: https://www.exeter.ac.uk/media/universityofexeter/humanresources/documents/learningdevelopment/the_change_curve.pdf

3 The special study "Digital School," from the year 2016, shows how disastrous the extent is (in German): http://initiatived21.de/publikationen/sonderstudie-schule-digital/

4 https://en.wikipedia.org/wiki/Noam_Chomsky

5 Please note that the division of conscious and subconscious mind is only a model. One that works very well, though.

6 Here is the TED Talk from Tony: https://www.youtube.com/watch?v=Cpc-t-Uwv1I

7 One of my favorite quotes from Tony Robbins is from a podcast he did with Tim Ferriss: "You either have results or a story you tell yourself every single day."

8 The dodo even has its own website: http://www.dodobird.net. The dodo became popular in business literature through my colleague Randy Pennington and his book, Make Change Work, which I highly recommend.

9 In my book, Think it. Do it. Change it., I have dealt with the topic of convictions in great detail.

10 In Think it. Do it. Change it., there's also a detailed overview on the subject of values.

11 Which I do once per year.

12 Always remember "Mindfulness, Baby!" because you can only change what you are aware of.

13 http://www.marriott.com/Multimedia/PDF/Marriott_Management_Philosophy.pdf

14 By this, I mean a tactic that is often used when the rational arguments have run out. The pressure is exerted on the emotional level, from which it is difficult to escape.

15 You can watch the original video clip here: https://www.youtube.com/watch?v=itFkfbs_hUc

16 More about Sobek: https://en.wikipedia.org/wiki/Sobek

17 https://en.wikipedia.org/wiki/Arthur_L._Williams_Jr.

18 By the way, I'm always very happy about nice reviews on Amazon. #WinkWink.

19 You can get a better understanding at https://youtu.be/FFx0moz5P4k

20 "This is your last chance. After this, there is no turning back. You take the blue pill—the story ends, you wake up in your bed and believe whatever you want to believe. You take the red pill—you stay in Wonderland and I show you how deep the rabbit hole goes." Statement by Morpheus in the film The Matrix.

21 I deal with this topic extensively in my book Think it. Do it. Change it.

22 https://en.wikipedia.org/wiki/Motivation

23 At least this would be my favorite leisure activity; please insert your favorite hobby here.

24 "Welcome to Lake Wobegon, where all the women are strong, all the men are good-looking, and all the children are above average." (From Garrison Keillor's book Lake Wobegon Days).

25 Real decisions involve commitment and stamina, as opposed to the popular "one should," "it would be nice if…," or "one would perhaps have to try it."

26 You can find the best Wowereit quotes here (in German): http://www.tagesspiegel.de/berlin/klaus-wowereit-die-besten-zitate-arm-sexy-schwul-mutig-dit-is-berlin/10610608.html

27 https://www.nytimes.com/2016/01/22/opinion/the-eight-second-attention-span.html

28 https://www.mpg.de/research/unconscious-decisions-in-the-brain

29 Gladstone Gander even has his own Wikipedia entry: https://en.wikipedia.org/wiki/Gladstone_Gander

30 https://en.wikipedia.org/wiki/Luck

31 https://en.wikipedia.org/wiki/Coincidence

32 In my book Attitüde—Erfolg durch die richtige innere Haltung (in German), I dedicated a whole chapter to the topic of attitude management.

33 Success Magazine: http://www.success.com/

34 I've just noticed that I seem to have a certain tendency toward formulas. After all, I've already written a whole book called Die Veränderungs-Formel, which means "The Change Formula."

35 If you really want a good laugh, then enter "Why can't you use phones on planes?" on YouTube. It's just great, and at the same time, kind of sad.

36 I'm fighting to change that, but that's a topic for another book at another time.

37 My complete Goals Model (including the reason why I am not a goals fanatic) can be found in my book Think it. Do it. Change it.

About the Author

Ilja Grzeskowitz is a global keynote speaker, author and economist. He was an executive manager for Germany's largest retail corporation Karstadt as well as for IKEA, before he started his own consulting company in 2009. He held guest lecturing positions at the Berlin School of Law and Economics and the SRH University in Berlin, and regularly travels around the world to research future trends and developments in the field of change management. As an author, he has published nine books (among them three bestsellers), which have been translated into ten different languages and sold hundreds of thousand copies worldwide.

Being nicknamed "Mr. Change" by his clients, Ilja inspires people to develop a changemaker mindset and supports organizations to establish a change culture that is based on purpose, diversity, and strong values. Among his clients are big brands like Accor, Allianz, Audi, Bayer, BASF, Biogen, BMW, Capri Sun, Continental, DPD, Kao, Lufthansa, Nespresso, Marriott, Mercedes, Pentax, P&G, Swiss, T-Mobile, Unitymedia, and Zara as well as traditional, middle-sized companies.

In his change programs, he combines real-world expertise with inspiring storytelling and scientific evidence, and, despite being German, rumor has it that he even has humor. If he is not speaking on a stage around the world, you might find him playing a round of golf, cheering for his favorite football teams (ManU and HSV) or enjoying a nice cup of coffee (always black and lots of it).

For more information, check out www.grzeskowitz.com